Education Through Worship

Also published by SCM Press

Background and Belief
R. J. Rees

New Ground in Christian Education
Harold Loukes

Religion and the Secondary School
Colin Alves

Religion and Slow Learners
K. E. Hyde

Religious Education in a Secular Setting
J. W. D. Smith

Sixth Form Religion
Edwin Cox

Sixth Form Worship
A. R. Bielby

Teenage Religion
Harold Loukes

A. R. BIELBY

Education Through Worship

SCM PRESS LTD

Abbreviations

The initials AV indicate the Authorized Version of the Bible, RSV the American Revised Standard Version, and NEB the New English Bible.

334 00363 6

First published 1969
by SCM Press Ltd
56 Bloomsbury Street London WC1

© *SCM Press Ltd 1969*

Printed in Great Britain by
Richard Clay (The Chaucer Press) Ltd
Bungay, Suffolk

CONTENTS

Preface		vi
I	Some First Things	1
	Assemblies 1–4: The Core of Religion	5
II	Education Through Worship	19
	Assembly 5: Worship and the Non-believer	24
	Assemblies 6–8: Thynke and Thanke	29
	Assemblies 9–12: Once-, Twice- & Oft-born	39
III	Working Together	49
	Assemblies 13–15: One Remove from Reality	52
	Assembly 16: A Catholic Spirit	61
	Assemblies 17–19: A Clear View	64
IV	Participation	73
	Assembly 20: Sikhism	77
	Assembly 21: Freedom	80
	Assemblies 22–25: Four French Authors	84
	Assemblies 26–28: Proverbs	97
V	Bible Themes	108
	Assemblies 29–31: Introduction to the Gospel	110
	Assemblies 32–37: Ezekiel	122
	Assemblies 38–40: The Four Evangelists	144
VI	Implications and Implementation	157
Acknowledgments		169

PREFACE

THIS is a practical book, based on work in a particular Sixth Form, and designed to be of service to those involved in school worship. It is a sequel to my earlier *Sixth Form Worship*.

It is, further, an argument *for* school worship, and as such it is based on two propositions.

The first is that judgments about the value of school worship cannot be based on past practice or on recollections of one's own early experience. No one would judge current teaching of mathematics in this way, yet changes in methods and outlook in religious education are as rapid as in mathematics, even though fewer people are fully equipped to effect them. It is important to know what is happening now.

The second is that religious education in schools is not ancillary to the work of the church. It stands in its own right on educational grounds because it meets basic needs of the growing person. Further, the teacher's success and standards of excellence lie within the area of his professional competence.

But because schools are set in a Christian tradition, the approach is fundamentally Christian, even though it remains open-ended.

The book is more than an argument: it is a demonstration. The worked-out assemblies do more than illustrate the text; they constitute part of the developing argument and they indicate approaches and attitudes which apply to all stages of school education.

I am deeply indebted to my former colleagues, Mr M. J. Rayner (for Assemblies 17–19) and Mr J. Gowans and his students (for Assemblies 22–25). Their contributions are instances of the very considerable goodwill I have found among masters when attempts are made to ensure that school worship is of educational value, goodwill without reference to whether they are 'believers' or 'non-believers'.

RONALD BIELBY

Huddersfield, 1969

I *Some First Things*

AT a time when the value of religious education is being questioned, and when investigations have shown how ineffective much teaching of Religious Studies is in our secondary schools, one way of contributing to the debate is to show what would be lost if schools were secularized. If Religious Studies (the term Religious *Instruction* is now misleading) ceased to be a legal requirement, the subject would almost certainly continue in secondary schools if only as an option. And it would, no doubt, continue among syllabuses for CSE and GCE. Pupils would not be *required* to study the subject any more than they are required to study Russian in schools in which Russian is an option. But it would not be sufficient to put Religious Studies among the options. Any education would be unbalanced if nothing were said of the role of religion in society and in the development of western European culture whether or not a specific course of Religious Studies were taken.

Religious education, however, includes more than teaching in the classroom; it includes the daily act of worship through which it is tied closely to the school as a community. One of the most important ways in which a school educates is through the impact on its pupils of the quality of its corporate life, the more important because largely unconscious. Visitors to schools are aware of it – it is made up of what is taken for granted about relationships between people; what is valued and approved, what is deplored and disapproved; the pattern of behaviour expected, whether of helpfulness and caring, or of competition and self-seeking; the achievements which get greatest praise; the nature of punishments and rewards. And this 'ethos' is linked with and is partly determined by the daily act of worship.

There could, of course, be assemblies without religious worship, and these could affect the tone of a school, for virtues are not the monopoly of the religious. Ethics can be an autonomous discipline; it need not lean on religion. Nevertheless it *is* necessary to ask what the good school owes to its daily act of worship, and what would be lost without it. For many it brings to a focus the pastoral concern of the school.

Perhaps assemblies of the present kind, with a religious element, could be optional, the whole school only being called together for important announcements? A start might be made in the 11–18 school with the Sixth Form. One might, experimentally, continue the compulsory assembly (with the usual safeguards) for the Main School and run a separate, but voluntary, assembly for Sixth Formers.

My own Sixth Form, when asked about this, quickly saw that a voluntary assembly for the Sixth Form would not work. Contracting out would become a status symbol, a mark of seniority; those attending would be toadying to the Head. It could not, in the nature of things, be a genuine choice; social pressures would be too great. They assumed that there would be an option of either attending assembly or of staying in their form-rooms – and the latter would provide a valuable last few minutes for homework. If the act of worship were conducted by various people, the popularity of the day's leader would vie with the urgency of completing the allotted task; and, in any case, a dance on the previous night could mean scant attendance at the next day's assembly.

I suggested that the only way to secure a genuine choice would be to run simultaneously two Sixth Form assemblies, one 'religious' and one 'secular'. The suggestion was received with consternation; it was clear that an option of this sort was not wanted. Objection to assembly was objection to regimentation and not primarily to religion. The determining factor for most would be the possible interest of the assembly and not the religious/secular alternative. Moreover, two assemblies would conflict with a recognized merit of one assembly; it makes for social cohesion.

It is a short step from this point to see that whatever would make a 'secular' assembly worth while could quite properly have a place in a 'religious' assembly; indeed it would *be* religious in the educational meaning of this term. One of the recurring embarrassments of religious education is the association of the term 'religion' with propaganda aspects of proselytizing faiths, and with the already-made-up mind which is dogmatic rather than open. The fact is that 'believer' and 'non-believer' alike have spiritual needs and education should help to meet their needs. It is not for nothing that one can speak of the religious atheist; indeed the thoughtful and searching Christian may have more in common with the thoughtful and searching agnostic than he has with those who never ask questions and who are content to be safe in the household of faith. There is a place, as we shall show, for such agnostics in the religious part of the daily assembly.

'I have always felt strongly that in an assembly of young people whose attendance is compulsory only damage will be done if a common body of belief is assumed, though, in a school, one hopes that something approaching a generally shared attitude might develop.' I agree with this comment of a neighbouring headmistress. The maintained school is set in a society which has no uniformity of belief or practice, but which nevertheless has a concern that its schools provide a wholesome environment for growth, psychological and emotional as well as intellectual. It is important, therefore, to discover the 'generally shared attitude' of those who are constructive in their attempt to provide such an environment. And here Christian and humanist must work together. I hope this book will show how such co-operation can begin.

An obvious difficulty arises from the general character of religious influence in a society. Religious worship tends to be conservative: there is a looking backwards to what Jude describes as 'the faith which was once for all delivered unto the saints'; emotions become attached to the old-established; there is implied an attitude of belonging to a group that possesses the only recipe for right living; the 'called-out' church is separate from the 'world'. Traditionalism may, in a school, produce carefully arranged acts of worship which seem to be valued, but which are, in fact, paternalistic, even hearty, in approach and which remain distant from the personal and philosophical problems which preoccupy the minds of thoughtful young people. Or, where the Head has no real interest in this part of his job, such acts become the conventional hymn–reading–prayer perfunctorily performed, the parts often independently selected without regard to unity of theme, so having little effect except inoculation against real religious search.

But just as there has always been the prophetic element in religion, and just as, in recent years, there has been in the churches experimentation in new forms of worship, so, in schools, there has been a growing endeavour to make school worship genuinely educational and thus significant to pupils. The rapid changes in society and changing standards have made the task urgent. It is here that we must look for the importance of the daily act of worship.

The worked-out assemblies of this book are designed to illustrate this contention. They do not form a course of assemblies; rather, they show the kind of approach which is being worked out in one school – a boys' grammar school, and in its Sixth Form, for the school has been able to run simultaneously two assemblies, one for the Main School and one for the Sixth Form. It seems better to work from the particularities of one situation so that applications of general principles can be seen. The whole field of school education, 5–18, is too wide for anything but the broadest generalizations. Problems are always particular. This book is based on experience with an academic Sixth Form.

Assemblies 1–4 are difficult; they were, in fact, based on teaching material. But they exemplify principles which will be developed later in the book. They define a stance. Following the assemblies are notes of explanation which should be read with them.

Assembly 1 (1 of 4)
The Core of Religion · 1

This assembly requires the use of a blackboard

Leader
Professor Christopher Zeeman of the Mathematics Institute of the University of Warwick, a leading topologist, has said that the solving of a mathematical problem is like the formation of stalactites and stalagmites. The mental activity is a double one: from the top, downwards, the stalactite; from the bottom, upwards, the stalagmite.

From the top downwards. You are asked to prove something. What does the result imply? It will be true if this . . ., and this will be true if this. . . . As the schoolmaster says: 'Work backwards from the result you want to prove.'

From the bottom upwards. What is your starting point? What do you know? What are you given, and what does this suggest? Each bit of information must be used. 'Make deductions from the data', the mathematics master says.

The solution comes with that moment of insight when these two, stalactite and stalagmite, link together. That, says Professor Zeeman, is how problems are solved. And it is remarkable how often problems in other fields yield to analysis of this kind.*

The method can be illustrated diagrammatically:

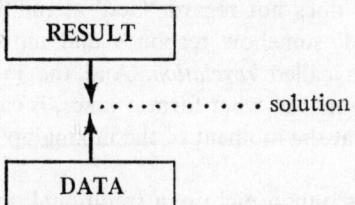

* A geometrical illustration is given on pp. 235, 236 in A. R. Bielby's *A New Geometry and Trigonometry* (Longmans, 1951). The problem is: Prove that the lines joining the mid-points of the opposite sides of a quadrilateral bisect each other. The stalactite aspect: We have to prove that two lines bisect each other. This suggests the diagonals of a parallelogram. It will be sufficient to prove that the four mid-points of sides are vertices of a parallelogram. The stalagmite aspect: Our information is about mid-points; this suggests the mid-point theorem and therefore triangles. How can we get triangles? By drawing a diagonal, All that remains is to link these two.

This double movement, of two things meeting and the meeting providing the moment of significance, supplies, for me, a picture of what is implied in worship. It enables us to see what is at the core of religion, whatever outward form religious activity may take. Whether or not we describe ourselves as religious it is important to know just what is central to religion, for without it, should we be in the opposition as it were, we may find ourselves tilting at windmills. And if we have faith, or are on the way to discovering it, it is well to know what is central lest we are put off by things which are secondary.

In worship, then, we assume two movements. We assume that there is a power outside man, greater than he is, existing apart from him, and, as it were, above him; and we assume that man seeks relationship with this power. Let us use the word 'God' for this spiritual power. The two movements are: from above downwards, and from man upwards. We may illustrate by modifying our earlier diagram:

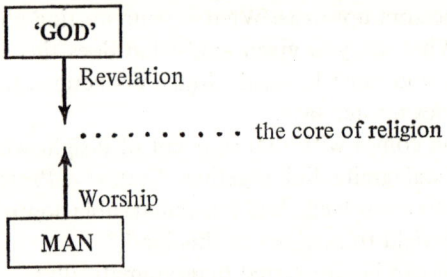

The worshipper does not regard 'God' as indifferent to him, he believes that 'God' somehow responds and moves towards man. This movement is called *revelation*. And the movement of man towards 'God', no matter what form it takes, is called *worship*. The core of religion is at the moment of the linking up of these two, this meeting place.

Of course this is only a picture, a traditional one at that; it uses words, abstractions. The reality does not lie in this analysis; it is of the whole man, deeply personal, a basic attitude. *Revelation* is like the stalactite, for the practice of religion implies belief in some power exterior to man; *worship* is like the stalagmite, it implies man's dependence on this bigger thing. And so religion is concerned with man's deepest response to life, the quality of his reaction to the sum total of his experience.

Let us pray

O Lord, help us to give thought to our basic attitudes, help us to get to know ourselves, lest in the enjoyment of activity we skim over the surface of life without ever reaching that fundamental commitment to truth in which our full maturity lies.

All   The grace of our Lord Jesus Christ,
                and the love of God,
                and the fellowship of the Holy Spirit,
            be with us all evermore.   Amen.

The Core of Religion · 2

Leader

The core of religion: perhaps you thought yesterday's analysis was too easy. You may have noticed that I called the picture a traditional one. It portrayed two movements:

> – the divine approach to man, which we called revelation, that is, the self-disclosure of God;
> – the human approach to the divine, which we called worship, and which includes prayer in all its kinds.

We said that at the meeting place of these two is the core of religion.

Why did I call this picture traditional, stalactites and stalagmites sound modern enough? Because it can be misunderstood, and in the same way as can much of the traditional language of faith. For it seems to separate 'God' from the world and make of him a 'supernatural being', above us in the heavens, related to the world as a watchmaker is to his watch.

Some of you may think this is the only meaning of the word 'God' – that he is, in fact, an external creator, one object among others in our world of ideas. And you doubt whether such a supernatural being exists.

Many Christians equally reject the language of supernaturalism; they would not say that Christians must believe in the supernatural. The terms 'natural' and 'supernatural' are outmoded and misleading. It was, indeed, as a protest against such language and the inadequacies of thinking that go with it that Dr John Robinson, until recently Bishop of Woolwich, wrote his famous book *Honest to God* (SCM Press, 1963). We shall hear a passage in which he quotes Paul Tillich.

Reading

Dr Robinson quotes Tillich as saying that God is not a projection 'out there', an Other beyond the skies, of whose existence we have to convince ourselves, but the Ground of our very being:

The name of this infinite and inexhaustible depth and ground of all being is *God*. That depth is what the word *God* means. And if that word has not much meaning for you, translate it, and speak of the depths of your life, of the source of your being, of your ultimate concern, of what you take seriously without any reservation. Perhaps, in order to do so, you must forget everything traditional that you have learned about God, perhaps even that word itself. For if you know that God means depth, you know much about him. You cannot then call yourself an atheist or unbeliever. For you cannot think or say: Life has no depth! Life is shallow. Being itself is surface only. If you could say this in complete seriousness, you would be an atheist; but otherwise you are not. He who knows about depth knows about God. (page 22)

Leader

The fundamental requirement of religion is to take life seriously – and joyfully. Yesterday's diagram, the stalactite and stalagmite, comprise a legitimate picture. We need many such pictures. Sometimes one, sometimes another, answers our needs. But pictures are not definitions; definitions elude us.

Let me repeat what I said yesterday; try to put it in the context of the quotation from Paul Tillich: Of course this is only a picture, a traditional one at that; it uses words, abstractions. The reality does not lie in this analysis; it is of the whole man, deeply personal, a basic attitude. . . . Religion is concerned with man's deepest response to life, the quality of his reaction to the sum total of his experience.

Let us pray

Almighty God, in whom we live and move and have our being, who hast made us for thyself so that we can find rest only in thee; grant us purity of heart and strength of purpose, so that no passion shall hinder us from knowing thy will, no weakness keep us from doing it. In thy light may we see light, and in thy service find our freedom and our strength, through Jesus Christ, our Lord.   Amen.

Prayers in Use at Uppingham School
(modified)

All   The grace of our Lord Jesus Christ,
and the love of God,
and the fellowship of the Holy Spirit,
be with us all evermore.   Amen.

The Core of Religion · 3

This assembly requires the use of a blackboard

Leader

The core of religion, we have seen, is at the place where man has to do with God – even though we find it hard to say what we mean by the word 'God'. Tillich means the Ground of our being.

Despite its dangers and limitations I should like to return to our illustration of two days ago. It enabled us to picture the relationship which is central to religion. I want to look at three variants of the main pattern.

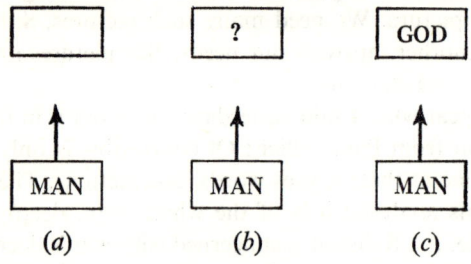

In each case Man is striving upwards; he has aspirations, he seeks to work out his ideals, he values supremely Goodness and Truth. He is not content with the philosophy 'Eat, drink and be merry, for tomorrow we die', nor with crude materialism.

But in (a) the heavens are empty. There is nothing which corresponds to, still less responds to, Man's strivings and yearnings. Anyway, why worry? Has he not resources within himself which will enable him to realize his own ideals? This is the attitude to life of some humanists. The word 'humanism' has many meanings, but when put in opposition to religion it means what diagram (a) says. Man is on his own in the universe. He must be self-sufficient; there is no Other.

Diagram (b) pictures the agnostic – not the attitude of indifference which does not know because it does not bother; but the uncertainty of him who has struggled to find out and who still cannot be sure. The picture is too simple; many who do believe in God are still largely agnostic. But for the real agnostic, as well as for those who are largely agnostic in their very faith, flatly to deny the existence of God would be to deny something very precious within themselves. You remember the man who said to Jesus, 'Lord, I believe; help thou mine unbelief' (*Mark* 9. 24, *AV*). God has to be grown into.

Diagram (*c*) represents bare theism – a belief in God, an infinite power; but it makes no difference to life. There is no 'revelation' – no speaking of God to the soul of man. It is an austere, cold, intellectual faith – the Deism of the seventeenth and eighteenth centuries.

We, ourselves, may be in one or other of these three pictures; or, however fumblingly, we may believe that there is the stalactite as well as the stalagmite: that the truth is nearer to our first drawing which we now repeat.

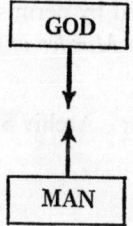

And, maybe, there is some significance in the fact that there could be no stalagmite were there not the stalactite. Our very thirst for God compels belief. As T. S. Eliot puts it in the words of the Chorus in *Murder in the Cathedral*; 'Those who deny Thee could not deny, if Thou didst not exist; and their denial is never complete, for if it were so, they would not exist.'

Instead of a prayer we shall hear part of the passage from *Murder in the Cathedral* from which the quotation comes. And then, after a short period of silence, and before announcements are made, we shall hear part of Bach's famous Toccata and Fugue in D minor.

Reading

We praise Thee, O God, for Thy glory displayed in all the creatures
  of the earth,

In the snow, in the rain, in the wind, in the storm; in all of Thy creatures, both the hunters and the hunted.

For all things exist only as seen by Thee, only as known by Thee, all things exist

Only in Thy light, and Thy glory is declared even in that which denies Thee; the darkness declares the glory of light.

Those who deny Thee could not deny, if Thou didst not exist; and their denial is never complete, for if it were so, they would not exist.

They affirm Thee in living; all things affirm Thee in living; the bird in the air, both the hawk and the finch; the beast on the earth, both the wolf and the lamb; the worm in the soil and the worm in the belly.

Therefore man, whom Thou hast made to be conscious of Thee, must consciously praise Thee, in thought and in word and in deed.

> Reprinted by permission of Faber & Faber Ltd.
> from *Murder in the Cathedral* by T. S. Eliot.

Recording

Band 1 on Side 1 of D.G.G. – Archiv SAPM 198002

Assembly 4

The Name of God

Copies of the words of the hymn should be issued to students for this assembly

Leader

Many ideas from the ancient world remain with us, embedded in language. For instance 'Hallowed be thy *name*', and again, 'In the *name* of the Father, and of the Son, and of the Holy Ghost'. In ancient thought the *name* of a person, and especially of a god, was more than a method of identification; it carried with it the person's character and authority. It was, therefore, important to know the name.

There is the story of the call of Moses; it followed the burning bush episode. He was to save Israel from Egypt, and there were difficulties: his own unfitness; but more, he did not know the name of his God.

Reading

Moses still pleaded with God: How if I appear before the Israelites with the message that the God of their fathers has sent me to them, and they ask me, What is his name? What answer shall I make? And God said to Moses, I am the God who IS; thou shalt tell the Israelites, THE GOD WHO IS has sent me to you. And he charged Moses again, That is what thou shalt tell the sons of Israel, that he who bears this name, the God of their fathers, Abraham, Isaac and Jacob has sent thee to them, and this is the name he shall be known by for ever; it shall stand recorded, age after age. *Ex.* 3. 13–15 *Knox*

Leader

'I am the God who IS', 'I AM THAT I AM', as the older version has it. Perhaps that doesn't tell you much, except this, that GOD cannot be contained (or encapsulated, as we might say) by a definition. He jumps out of the categories of our thinking; he can never be one object among others in the world of our thinking.

Why, even in science, fundamental questions such as 'What *is* gravitation?' and 'What *is* light?' are impossible to answer. We have to be content with *models*, with knowing how things work rather than with knowing what they *are*. And, in a sense, we know God only by what he does. In seeking to understand and interpret our experience we deal with Him who is; 'the Ground of our being', in Tillich's phrase. 'Thou shalt tell the Israelites, THE GOD WHO IS has sent me to you.'

One of the difficulties in the way of our accepting a religious view of life is the persistence of crude, rigid notions which fix thought at a primitive level. Many hymns, for instance, perpetuate out-dated theology as well as out-dated psychology. We have seen, this week, how misleading are the old terms 'natural' and 'supernatural'; we can no longer use them.

I suppose that many people have become atheists to escape from a caricature of religion, since all they see is hard and defined, and has in it no room for their growth.

This is why poetry and the arts are often of more value than theological formulations. And, for many, the drama of the sacraments. John Wesley, in one of his great translations from the German, speaks of

> Essential life's unbounded sea.

We shall hear the hymn; I do not think you will find its thinking hard and defined. It will be sung to a tune by Luther as arranged by Bach.

Hymn (Tune: *Vom Himmel Hoch* (*Erfurt*). Nos. 126 and 42 in the Methodist Hymn Book.)

> O God, Thou bottomless abyss!
>   Thee to perfection who can know?
> O height immense! What words suffice
>   Thy countless attributes to show?
>
> Unfathomable depths Thou art;
>   O plunge me in Thy mercy's sea!
> Void of true wisdom is my heart;
>   With love embrace and cover me.
>
> Eternity Thy fountain was,
>   Which, like Thee, no beginning knew;
> Thou wast ere time began his race,
>   Ere glowed with stars the ethereal blue.

Unchangeable, all-perfect Lord,
   Essential life's unbounded sea,
What lives and moves, lives by Thy word;
   It lives, and moves, and is from Thee.

Greatness unspeakable is Thine,
   Greatness, whose undiminished ray,
When short-lived worlds are lost, shall shine
   When earth and heaven are fled away.

Ernst Lange, 1650–1727;
tr. by John Wesley, 1703–91

Let us pray

O God, the living God, who hast put thine own eternity in our hearts, and hast made us to hunger and thirst after thee: Satisfy, we pray thee, the instincts which thou hast implanted in us, that we may find thee in life, and life in thee; through Jesus Christ our Lord.

From Milner-White & Briggs, *Daily Prayer*,
OUP, 1941

Now to the King of all worlds, immortal, invisible, the only God, be honour and glory for ever and ever. *Amen.*

I *Tim.* 1. 17

NOTES ON ASSEMBLIES 1–4

1. *The setting*

These four assemblies presuppose established practice, and therefore an audience ready to listen, knowing the kind of thing to expect. Audio-equipment should be of good quality (we use stereo equipment with two Leak Sandwich speakers), and music should justify attention as students enter. The setting should be dignified and the production impeccable. There should be no sense of haste; use should be made of silences; and the departure should be quiet and also with a background of music.

2. *Treatment of the theme*

Because they are expositional these assemblies owe more to the leader than many will. Systematic and exhaustive treatment of a theme is neither possible nor desirable in assembly. I have tried, by a series of vignettes, to stir the mind and imagination, and so introduce ideas and extend understanding. Putting together material for an assembly is like writing a sonnet – there is need for taut selection.

Students will be amused that the headmaster has dragged in his specialism (mathematics) – fair enough!

3. *The student's part*

In general more student participation will be expected than here, though the four-part singing in Assembly 4 will require rehearsal. Unless it can be done well, with clear enunciation, it should not be done, or should be sung solo, or even read. But assemblies *should* involve both students and teaching staff; assembly belongs to them.

4. *Manner*

Care should be taken to avoid any kind of talking-down, or of moral pressure that might make the non-believer uncomfortable;

there should be no preaching. Confusion about religious terms should be recognized. But the comment of one Sixth Former, 'I don't believe in God, but I do believe that there is something behind things', is not just confusion; it expresses dissatisfaction with theism. John A. T. Robinson says 'representation of God as a Person is the source, or at any rate the occasion, of great stumbling. . . . It produces in many sheer unbelief' (*Exploration into God*, SCM Press, 1967, p. 136). Yet for others it is a matter of faith and of great comfort. One has to speak at many levels in assembly.

5. *Follow-up*

Morning worship might well provoke subsequent discussion in the classroom, say, in the General Studies or Religious Studies classes. Masters, anticipating future lessons, might even suggest themes for assembly which they can follow up.

Assembly 1 provokes a question which could be asked in two ways:

either (*a*) In what ways has God revealed himself?
or (*b*) What forms of revelation have men believed in?

Style (*b*) is the right one for a maintained school; (*a*) is for the church group.

Assembly 2 raises questions of terminology, yet old terms can scarcely be avoided. The religious studies teacher might compare the use of 'natural', 'supernatural' with the scientific terms 'good', 'perfect', 'law'. Few scientists are troubled by the moral implications of 'a *good* conductor', 'a *perfect* gas'; or by the overtones of obligation in Boyle's *law*. But some people still think of 'laws' as *controlling* events.

Assembly 3 might well illustrate the adage: seek simplicity, then suspect it. The mind requires a simple framework if it is even to begin to grasp complex phenomena; subsequently, elaboration is possible. Just so Boyle's law gives way to Van der Waals' equation. But the 'simplicity' may be a false start (as, in Botany, classifying plants by the colours of their flowers); it is important not to get into a cul-de-sac.

6. *Why no prayer in Assembly 3?*

It depends on what you mean by prayer! A simple theistic religion conceives of God as a Being in a spiritual realm, and of prayer as talking to him. But there are other ways of thinking. Some schoolmasters who care for the spiritual growth of students cannot use the formal style of public prayer. It is not that 'thees' and 'thous' sound unreal; it is that they cannot personalize their spiritual awareness. The leader of assembly who can use the traditional form of prayer should sometimes do without it so that these colleagues, when taking assembly, will not be odd men out. There will certainly be many senior boys who share their outlook.

7. *Valuing tradition*

The use of the Old Testament, and of known prayers, and of a Wesley hymn, in a group of assemblies which are radical in outlook, is deliberate. Wisdom was not born yesterday; Moses was an existentialist over 3000 years ago!

II *Education Through Worship*

MORE is expected of a school than instruction; assembly stands as a symbol of this wider concern. Despite the current tendency to dispense with symbols, they have an important place in life. At deeper moments they express what words cannot say; as part of normal courtesies they preserve attitudes that could ill be lost.

Even a conventional assembly is an acknowledgment of values that go beyond selfish materialism. But a school's assemblies should not be conventional; they should be seen as a major educational influence in its life, affecting attitudes, and making explicit those basic values which determine standards expected in personal living. They should, in fact, be educational.

A possible reaction to this, and to the title of the chapter, is a feeling of its impropriety. Should worship be *used* to serve *our* ends? This may be a purist's objection: worship, the chief end of man, should never be a means for anything, however worthy. Or it may be a humanist's objection: you should not bring in the idea of a god to buttress morality, it savours of indoctrination – brainwashing a captive audience.

The first of these objections cannot be sustained. Public worship involves more than 'adoration' (one of its elements). Every church has a pulpit; older churches are full of teaching devices in stained glass, pictures, and symbols; 'the ministry of the word' is part of the original commission, 'teaching them to observe all that I have commanded you' (*Matt.* 28. 20). Nevertheless, the point of this objection should be taken. Worship implies acknowledgment of an Absolute, and therefore of a fundamental commitment which is binding, and which excludes the attitude of 'Well, it's good for them' – treating the act of worship as a performance or a prophylactic.

The second objection has to be faced. But 'indoctrinate' is the wrong word for what we seek to do. Teaching would be a dull thing if every teacher was expected to be neutral on every issue – impossible, anyway, for selection of material implies making value judgments. And though pupils are taught to think for themselves, they know very well that the teacher regards Shakespeare as greater than the sports page writer in the local newspaper, and that he *is* greater. Even the heuristic methods of Nuffield science prescribe the kind of experiment from which inferences *can* be drawn. There is no point in repeating Faraday's 999 negative experiments when we know that only the thousandth was significant. We guide children along lines which make their own growth possible. It is not indoctrination when, fundamental to your approach, is a respect for pupils as individuals in their own right. They are not clay to be moulded, for clay is inert. Their critical faculties are not to be inhibited so that, by a kind of brainwashing, they come to accept common value judgments in literature and in the arts and in science. To be educated, they *must* learn to judge for themselves; from knowledge and not from ignorance.

But does worship imply an elaborate traditional orthodoxy, a metaphysical system which is no longer acceptable to thinking men? There have been many orthodoxies, many ways of expressing man's spiritual awareness, but with a Christian heritage our starting point is to draw on that heritage. It is not a crabbed narrow constraint, but a starting point for our own exploration, and itself something to explore. We think of this heritage not as propositional in character, but as pointing to a way of experiencing.

School worship can do this; it can be open-ended; it can respect the attitudes of both the sincere believer and the sincere non-believer. It does, however, require serious intent, and a capacity and readiness for growth.

There is a sense in which schools should reflect the pluralism of belief and practice in the world around them. But not all belief; not all practice. The 'commonly shared attitude' of a school should have a place for what is best in both religious and humanist attitudes – there is much in both to avoid. But humanist and Christian *can* work together.

A large part of the humanist's hesitation about assembly and about religious education in schools arises from the public image of the church and its unexplained use of language. The disenchantment can readily be understood, but it remains a handicap to be overcome.

Monica Furlong, in *With Love to the Church* (Hodder & Stoughton, 1965), says 'There are many Christians who go to church for lack of any better way to show loyalty to their beliefs, and many more who stay away, but who find the services, the simple teaching about prayer and meditation, the formula of confession, almost meaningless, or worse, a threat to their integrity' (p. 74). Despite the fact that most denominations are seeking revision of their orders of worship most services remain tired, slow-moving, and with the air of old successes repeated till they have become tedious. The fact is that what is real to people is that on which their understanding and insights grow, and here psychology proves more helpful than theology, and discussion more than sermons. People go outside the church for what is new and exciting and liberating to their spirits. Churches have always been laggard in accepting new knowledge whether in physical and biological sciences or in psychology or in biblical criticism. In most subjects in school, and certainly in science, the pupil is aware that two years hence he will know more than he knows now; there is better stuff coming. Expectancy is part of the excitement of learning. Only rarely does he find this kind of anticipation in church. Instead, emotions are tied to nursery ideas by hymns and practices which fixate thinking and so inhibit growth. Yet it is what people grow on that they value.

To a large extent this is linked with the use of language. Inevitably, in a historical religion, language and thought forms go back many centuries. It is necessary to explain old usage, the way in which spiritual insights were expressed in terms of the thinking of the day; necessary to translate old symbols and myths, and ideas couched in terms of old cosmologies, into language consistent with twentieth-century thinking. But this is rarely done in any systematic way in our churches; familiarity with traditional terminology, and willingness to use it, are often deemed enough. Nevertheless, speaking of the Roman Catholic Church, E. E. Y. Hales writes, in *Pope John and his Revolution* (Eyre & Spottiswoode, 1965), 'The Church cannot live effectively in the world save by clothing herself in the garments of the living contemporary culture, . . . It may, indeed, be more important that she should so clothe herself than that she should reform her government – though the two matters are, of course, related' (p. 204).

The official language of religion gelled in a pre-scientific era and carries assumptions which are no longer tenable. Phrases such as 'He descended into hell' become as empty as 'above the bright blue sky'.

Liturgical use of statements once deemed central, but now either not understood, or not fully believed, or peripheral, or irrelevant, or merely serving to confirm a nostalgia for an idealized personal or historic past – these statements repeatedly used, despite conscious attempts to get to their inner meaning, create a sense of unreality; they are too far from issues which divide men today and from the affirmations which a Christian would now have to make to define his position. Yet they are the phrases, coupled with the sentimentalism of hymns (Father, lead me day by day Ever in Thine own sweet way), which the young are asked to accept. The language remains unexplained, its inadequacies never hinted at. Adults uncritically adopt it, and its saccharinity, thinking thereby that they are helping the young. And all the time it is the empiricism of science which is their daily bread! Why should every child in adolescence be expected to recapitulate in his own thinking the intellectual changes of the centuries of Western Europe since the Renaissance? And why should he be expected to do it without mentors from the Christian church? That is often what we do expect when religion is associated with outdated language – a geocentric world view, a universe of manageable dimensions of both space and time, and a simple supplementation of natural law by revelation.

One consequence of the failure of churches to *teach* the faith in the modern idiom is that the 'outsider', and those who form the 'wastage' at twelve from Sunday Schools, have curiously naïve ideas of what Christianity is about. There is a persistent literalism which is difficult to eradicate. I remember a neighbour, who described herself as an atheist, saying to me with surprise 'You, a Christian, cutting your grass on a Sunday!' I expostulated that I was not a sabbatarian, but this was not enough. 'If you are a Christian, at least you should confine your cutting on a Sunday to the back garden where you'll not be seen.' So was hypocrisy in the churchgoer assumed! And there are similar misunderstandings about the so-called propositions of religion, even to 'You must believe the whale swallowed Jonah, if you are a Christian.' This literalism is now most often believed of Christians by those who are outside the churches or are peripheral to them. It refers not only to the bible, but to doctrine also. The consequent misunderstandings are very pervasive, and the humanist who accepts them will find it hard to co-operate with the Christian in a school's acts of worship.

It is often as though the objector to religion wants to retain the target which he attacks even though a bogus one. He resents being robbed of it, for then the 'believer' is not true to his belief! He needs to keep his grievances and the sense that he knows just where the religious person stands, for this confirms him in his superiority in not falling for that kind of self-deception. He needs the stereotype. And it is the church's reluctance to re-word its own faith which has provided it!

There are many cul-de-sacs in spiritual growth; the humanist may be in one and the Christian in another, and dead language may justify both! The purpose of religious education is *not* to secure the acceptance of doctrines couched in traditional language; it is to keep the student open to growth and to develop his sensitiveness to the deep things of the spirit. If the Christian himself is seeking, if he is grappling with contemporary problems, and if the humanist is doing the same, there can be no mutual recriminations, no annoyances that either is not true to type; they do not take up prepared positions and battle with each other. There will be dialogue, but it will not be debate. There will be mutual respect, and readiness to learn from each other and share insights, and the desire each to do what he can in a common task.

The meaning of this for assembly is evident. The church may sometimes seem to be apologetic and on the defensive, but assembly must not be. Assembly must be positive, constructive, and forward-looking, so that it becomes part of the school's life which nourishes the spirit and makes explicit what is the ground of its being. And this is why consideration of the contemporary religious scene is necessary. Assembly must avoid taking for granted what the churchman finds familiar in language and thought-forms; it must approach commonplace religious ideas with freshness for the uninitiated, and with clarity for the misinformed, beginning, as it were, *ab initio*, yet using the often misconstrued residual Christian ideas. The assemblies which follow pick up some of these points. Assembly 5 was fourth in a series on Patterns of Worship in which three masters described their forms of service and what they valued; one was a Quaker, one a Methodist, and one a Roman Catholic. Notes of explanation follow this assembly and also succeeding series. Assemblies 6–8 draw on church inscriptions; Assemblies 9–12 on biblical/psychological themes.

Assembly 5

Worship and the Non-believer

Leader

During this week we have been thinking of worship in three modes, Quaker, Methodist, and Catholic. But what of those who cannot worship because they do not believe? They, too, have spiritual needs. And what of those for whom the outward forms of worship, whether Quaker, Free Church, or Roman Catholic, do not answer to their real needs? Where are they to find spiritual nourishment?

Some find none; some do not recognize their own needs. What *is* true is that any problem of art or life, looked at deeply, puts you on ground shared by religion. At some point, in some way, we have to meet the requirements of the Greek adage: KNOW THYSELF.

I want us to hear some verses written by modern-school children who, in their English classes, were learning to feel and write about personal things. They were not saying the things supposed to be expected by teachers; somehow, conditions had been created in which sincerity became possible. If there is pathos in them, that is my selection.

Readings (from Jack Beckett, *The Keen Edge*, Blackie & Son, 1965. Nos. 75, 50, 87, 77, 96; the spelling is the children's).

1. About not passing the 11+.

> The postman tramped methodically on his daily rounds,
> His footsteps drawing nearer and nearer.
> My heart thumped against my ribs
> As I listened intently for the rattling
> of the door knocker, as the letters settled down
> on the highly polished floor
> Like nestling birds.
>
> But I waited in vain there were no letters
> Just the footsteps of the postman
> echoing in my head
> as they got fainter and fainter.

I turned away miserabele and downcast,
I had failed to pass the examination,
I was a failure.

2. About being 13.

> When I look out of my window
> And see young children play and fight
> I feel as if I were old and aged
> and long to join them.
> But yet inside me I wish to be
> about 18 or 19 years of age
> and go to dances and cinemas and clubs
> But at 13 years of age
> Theres not much I can do
> but sit inside and watch and wait
> for things one wants to do.

3. About having no father.

> Ho God
> Help me to get
> Over things
> That worry
> Me so, Help me
> As I get older.
>
> I feel that I get
> Left out of things.
> Over children
> Have fathers
> But I have not.
> They talk about
> The trips they take
> With there parents
> But I say
> I am happy
> But deep down inside me
> I feel hurt.
> And it hurts more
> And more all the time.
> Ho God please help me.

>   My mother says
>   She will marry
>   But sometimes
>   She jokes about it
>   I laugh
>   But deep down inside me
>   I feal hurt
>   But I do not show it.
>   Ho, God please help me.

4. About living in rooms.

   > I am a boy I have not had
   > a very good life
   > Me and my mom and sister
   > live in rooms.
   >
   > A long time ago my Dad
   > hit my mom
   >
   > She left him
   > three years later he die
   >
   > I hope to go to work
   > and get out of rooms
   >
   > It is not very pleasant
   > to live in rooms.

5. About wanting to tell someone.

   > There are some things in life
   > Which I would rather keep to myself.
   > I feel I would like to forget these
   > But something urges me to put them down on paper.
   > I sometimes feel very depressed and would like to cry.
   > I feel very hateful at times
   > And try to pull myself together
   > But it does no good.
   > Feelings of wanting to tell someone
   > Whirl through my mind.
   > The little feelings down beyond me,
   > I am afraid to tell anyone about them.
   > I am afraid they will laugh.

Leader

Such writing is therapeutic – it heals; it releases the pus of resentment or self-pity. And this is what worship does – enables a man to look at himself, warts and all, in the light of his ideals, of God.

You remember the phrase in Psalm 23, 'He restoreth my soul'? That is what it means.

Let us pray

Our prayer is a meditation.

Lord, help us to be able to be honest with ourselves.

Some people pay money to psychiatrists
> to get a sympathetic professional ear;
> – without it they cannot learn to accept themselves.

Some people can be honest with themselves before God, needing
> no other person to open their hearts to.
> They learn to see themselves as they are, and,
> like the prodigal son of old who came to himself,
> learn that they, too, are accepted of their Father.
> Forgiveness, reconciliation, are words with meaning.

Some of us are so tied up with ourselves that we cannot
> disentangle ourselves enough to be honest.
> We run away from ourselves, and find we take ourselves
> with us.
> Neither action, nor phantasy; neither business, nor
> pleasure, provides escape.

Help us, O Lord, to be genuine people
> able to be straight with ourselves, and with others.

And keep alive in us ideals, reverence, and readiness to grow
> towards what is good.   Amen.

NOTES ON ASSEMBLY 5

1. The contents and character of this assembly depended on the earlier three (not given here). Together they comprise an example of team teaching. Each master heard what the others had to say, and each found it hard to limit himself to the allotted time!

2. It is important that the headmaster is present, and is seen to be joining in, when not conducting assembly himself. He does not have a day off! Not only does this enhance the value of assembly in the eyes of the students; it helps the headmaster to judge reactions and needs.

3. The reading of the verse should be dry and unsentimental, though sympathetic. Few boys can do this.

4. The words 'Let us pray' are accepted as a signal to stand. This prayer-meditation gets very near to preaching! There is a striding edge between what is acceptable and what would be resented, and the leader must know and feel *with* his students. Prayer should not be used for passing on moral advice! The leader (whether the headmaster or not) should be able to identify himself with the various attitudes of students ('all things to all men', I *Cor.* 9. 22).

Assembly 6 (1 of 3)
Thynke and Thanke

Leader

When you motor on the A1 from the north to London, a few miles after by-passing Grantham, you go through the village of Great Ponton. A stone's throw from the south-bound lane, at the east, lies a handsome square-towered church whose weathervane is shaped like a fiddle. It is worth while to make a break in your journey to look at the church. On three sides of the tower you will notice in Gothic lettering the inscription

THYNKE AND THANKE GOD OF ALL.

The tower dates from the sixteenth century. Thynke and Thanke was a not uncommon inscription; it is also found on fonts. Thynke: T, H, Y, N, K, E; Think and thank.

What does it mean for us? Some people put it like this:

'Sacred Song' (A choir of several voices)

> When upon life's billows you are tempest-tost,
> When you are discouraged, thinking all is lost,
> Count your many blessings, name them one by one,
> And it will surprise you what the Lord hath done.
>
>> Count your blessings, name them one by one,
>> Count your blessings, see what God hath done;
>> Count your blessings, name them one by one,
>> And it will surprise you what the Lord hath done.

Leader

'Count your many blessings' – this is what the old Sankey-type hymn says, the equivalent of the modern religious pop song. Most of us don't do this very often. Advertisements make us aware of what we haven't got; we take for granted what we have. We think of those more fortunate than we are, or of those ahead of us in our careers, and we covet what they have; sometimes we envy them. We rarely 'thynke and thanke God of all'.

And yet to be thankful is a wholesome attitude to life.

Perhaps we only consider material goods, things that money can buy. The 'count your blessings' idea seems a bit selfish. It has something of the 'I'm all right, Jack' attitude. We think of the poverty and distress in the world, and then 'think and thank' sounds a bit self-centred, doesn't it?

How else can we think? Is it possible to be thankful and not be selfish? Surely it is. We can be thankful and therefore more concerned with the less fortunate; indeed some of you are.

But there is another way of thinking and thanking God of all. Man is the only animal who knows what is going on. He not only lives; he knows that he lives. His capacity to reflect on his situation has made philosophy possible, science possible, religion possible. No cow admires a sunset; no sheep says its prayers; no dog proves Pythagoras's theorem. Man is special in creation, 'made in the image of God', the old myth says; special because he *can* change the face of the earth.

Think, then, and be thankful: you are not blind, contained by the inexorable processes of evolution; you can stand outside the process and act, and do something when things go wrong. You are no puppet, but a man. Paul, the apostle, puts it more strongly: a fellow-worker with God.

For our reading we shall hear the passage from which this phrase comes, in Paul's first letter to the Corinthians; he begins by reproving partisanship, sectarianism.

Reading

While there is jealousy and strife among you, you are living on the purely human level of your lower nature. When one says, 'I am Paul's man', and another, 'I am for Apollos', are you not all too human?

After all, what is Apollos? What is Paul? We are simply God's agents in bringing you to the faith. Each of us performed the task which the Lord allotted to him: I planted the seed, and Apollos watered it; but God made it grow. Thus it is not the gardeners with their planting and watering who count, but God, who makes it grow. Whether they plant or water, they work as a team, though each will get his own pay for his own labour. We are God's fellow-workers; and you are God's garden.

I *Cor.* 3. 3b–9 *NEB*

Let us pray

Thynke and thanke God of all.
Please respond with the phrase: We give thee thanks, O God.

For all that we enjoy in the world, both its beauty and its bounty:

> *We give thee thanks, O God.*

For home and friendships, and the power to appreciate and love in return:

> *We give thee thanks, O God.*

For the truth we are learning, and the work we hope to do:

> *We give thee thanks, O God.*

For the kingdom of God for which we are bidden to pray, and for the call to be fellow-workers with thee and each other for the extension of that kingdom:

> *We give thee thanks, O God.*

We think and thank God of all.   Amen

The Lord's Prayer

All   The grace of our Lord Jesus Christ,
and the love of God,
and the fellowship of the Holy Spirit,
be with us all evermore.   Amen.

Assembly 7 (2 of 3)

'Go About Your Business'

Leader

Our thinking today will start from a blunt inscription, 'Go about your business', found on the sundial over the porch of the church at Clare, in Suffolk.

The village of Clare was an ancient stronghold; from it, through the family of the Earls of Clare, Clare College in Cambridge derives its name. It was a centre for cloth in the Middle Ages, and for corn when the railway was built. It is now a quiet village with a spacious, dignified, and plain church – like many in East Anglia. Inside the porch the stone is much worn. 'There is no local stone in Suffolk,' says Justin Brooke of Clopton Hall, not far away, 'and those inhabitants in old times who wanted to sharpen their knives and tools brought them to the church porch for sharpening, thus wearing away the stone.'

But what of the inscription 'Go about your business'? I want to link it with compassion, the love of our fellow men, that comes from understanding how they feel.

Adolescence, as you know, brings for some a difficult period of self-consciousness. Many of you know what shyness means and the blushing that follows social gaucherie or even social uncertainty. Shyness arises from concern with the impression *you* are giving though, often, others are not thinking of you at all. Such self-consciousness can be a disabling thing, spoiling the day both for you and for others. It stems from looking inwards, thinking of oneself and not of what is external to oneself. It would be a hard thing to say that shyness is a form of selfishness; it seems scarcely to be under your control. Yet a remedy is deliberately to think of others, of how *you* can put them at their ease – for this involves looking outwards, away from your own reactions.

I want us to hear a relevant passage from one of Bertrand Russell's books. He is thinking of the introvert and the extrovert.

Reading

The reading is from Bertrand Russell's book *The Conquest of Happiness* (Allen & Unwin, 1930, p. 160).

There were once upon a time two sausage machines, exquisitely constructed for the purpose of turning pig into the most delicious sausages. One of these retained his zest for pig and produced sausages innumerable; the other said: 'What is pig to me? My own works are far more interesting and wonderful than any pig.' He refused pig and set to work to study his inside. When bereft of its natural food, his inside ceased to function, and the more he studied it, the more empty and foolish it seemed to him to be. All the exquisite apparatus by which the delicious transformation had hitherto been made stood still, and he was at a loss to guess what it was capable of doing. This second sausage machine was like a man who has lost his zest, while the first was like the man who has retained it. The mind is a strange machine which can combine the materials offered to it in the most astonishing ways, but without materials from the external world it is powerless, and unlike the sausage machine it must seize its material for itself, since events only become experiences through the interest that we take in them: if they do not interest us, we are making nothing of them. The man, therefore, whose attention is turned within finds nothing worthy of his notice, whereas the man whose attention is turned outward can find within, in those rare moments when he examines his soul, the most varied and interesting assortment of ingredients being dissected and recombined into beautiful or instructive patterns.

Leader

'Go about your business' – Perhaps it is an oblique use of the injunction; but it is sound advice for the shy and diffident. Think of others, not of your own feelings; this will help you to escape from self-consciousness. Look outwards; go about your business.

And what then? There will come a time when you will be glad of your own difficulties, for through them you will be able to feel a greater sympathy for others, entering into how they feel. And this is a large part of compassion – loving one's neighbour.

Let us pray

Lord, help us to look upward and outwards, not downward and inwards. Amen.

Ihesu Be Our Speed

Leader

At the head of Wharfedale, one of the loveliest of the Yorkshire dales, lies Hubberholme church, the last church up the valley. Originally a forest chapel, it dates from the twelfth century, though the porch bears a seventeenth-century date. An old cracked bell, replaced by two new bells in 1904, stands in the church. On it are inscribed Queen Elizabeth I's coat-of-arms, the date 1601, and the inscription IHESU BE OUR SPEED.

'Jesus be our Speed': that is our theme for today.

Our *speed*; the word is used when we wish people God-speed; when we speed them on their way. It means success, prosperity, faring well. IHESU BE OUR SPEED: Jesus be our success; Jesus fare us well.

Right at the centre of Christianity is the enigmatic figure of Jesus Christ. However much Christian opinion may differ on other things Christians do not differ on the centrality which they give to Jesus. However arid and abstruse much Christian theology may sound to modern ears its principal task is 'to endeavour to explain the significance of Jesus Christ, the knowledge of God's nature and purpose which he makes possible, and the consequences for human life which follow from his appearance in history'. IHESU BE OUR SPEED is the kernel of the Christian faith.

And now for a parallel with Physics. You will know that we speak of classical physics, and that this has given way to modern physics. The Michelson and Morley experiment might be taken as a dividing line; Einstein belongs to the modern era. Classical physics, that is Newtonian physics, is associated with Euclidean geometry. Somewhere in the universe was a fixed frame of reference. And this classical physics with its fixed axes and absolute velocities still has a place; it is the basis of most mechanical engineering. But the change has come; Newton's world picture has broken down.

Much the same sort of thing marks recent theology. We can speak of classical theology with its elaborate systematizing. It seemed absolute and closed, yet it has been forced open. The word 'demythologizing' bears witness to this, and among recent names, Tillich, Bonhoeffer and Harvey Cox. But it is the old systematization, not the Christian faith itself, that has failed. Certainly these three theologians believe that Christian faith meets the needs of the man of today.

And for many simpler folk, too, IHESU BE OUR SPEED is still the test, the touchstone. Anything inconsistent with what he has shown of the kingdom of God cannot be true; in him is depth, understanding, the way to the Father.

Those of you who know the gospels will remember how John summarizes this in the great claim: 'I am the way, and the truth, and the life; no one comes to the Father, but by me' (*John* 14. 6). No wonder Christians sometimes begin worship by saying

> Lord, thou hast called us by thy name,
> and we are thine.

Instead of a prayer we shall hear a poem by Alice Meynell with the title 'I am the way', and this will be followed by the singing of a hymn – you may know the words, translated from twelfth-century Latin; the tune dates from 1709. (Alternatively a recording of *Jesu, joy of man's desiring* might be used.)

Reading

> Thou art the Way.
> Hadst Thou been nothing but the goal
>   I cannot say
> If Thou hadst ever met my soul.
>
> I cannot see –
> I, child of process – if there lies
>   An end for me,
> Full of repose, full of replies.
>
> I'll not reproach
> The road that winds, my feet that err.
>   Access, approach
> Art Thou, Time, Way, and Wayfarer.

Solo

Number 547, verses 1–5, in *Songs of Praise*, to the tune *King's Norton*:

> Jesu! the very thought of thee
> With sweetness fills my breast.

(It is important, if the words are to be acceptable, that this tune be used. If the school pattern allows it, and if there is available a boy treble who can enunciate clearly and sing sincerely, then he might be 'borrowed' for this assembly.)

NOTES ON ASSEMBLIES 6–8

1. *Why groups of three or four assemblies?*
I have found that variety is essential to keep assembly alive. The week is organized to give a three-day grouping on Monday, Tuesday, and Wednesday, with the possibility of an extra assembly in a series on Friday. Thursday is used for House prayers.

2. *Use of church inscriptions*
Assemblies 6–8 do more than bring diverse topics within a common formula. They attempt to create an interest in churches by out-flanking the blockages created by anti-ecclesiastical prejudices. The method should not be overdone, and, when done, should include churches of local interest. I have used a Latin tag carved on a schoolmaster's chair bearing the date 1664 to be found near the pulpit in the parish church at Hope in Derbyshire. *Ex torto ligno non fit mercurius:* 'You cannot make a scholar out of a block of wood.' What headmaster could resist that? Another, of personal interest though grim, is engraved on the sundial of a 1837 chapel in the village of Bielby in the East Riding of Yorkshire: 'BOAST not thyself of tomorrow for on thine eyelids is the shadow of death.'

3. The Sankey-type hymn of Assembly 6, though found in most mission hymnbooks, is not well known nowadays. It can be enjoyed. The use of responses in prayers is designed to involve the students. I have not found them very effective, perhaps because not used regularly enough to be expected.

4. Assembly 7 affords with Assembly 6 an interesting link which is not developed here. The embarrassing but decreasing self-consciousness of Assembly 7 is a small price to pay for the enriching and increasing self-awareness of Assembly 6. 'Go about your business'

may be biblical though I have not found it as a translation of Paul's phrase 'Mind your own affairs' (I *Thess.* 4. 11) which is embedded in a paragraph about love of the brethren. The short quotation in the Leader's section is from *Suffolk Prospect* by Justin and Edith Brooke (Faber, 1963).

5. Assembly 8 calls for follow-up. The quotation about the principal task of Christian theology is taken from the recent London Agreed Syllabus *Learning for Life* (ILEA 1968, p. 16).

Paul's Conversion

Leader

During this week we turn to the bible, to the New Testament. To understand its stories is to understand ourselves – how *our* minds work.

I want us to look at the growth of the early church, and at how men grew in understanding. We begin with an easy case, with what is called Paul's conversion: Paul, who persecuted the church, and then became the great apostle to the Gentiles.

What is conversion? – apart from the meaning given to it in religion. It is a psychological term for a kind of delayed action, and then a sudden change. It can happen in any province in which we are deeply involved – in politics, in personal relations, in religion (either *to* it, or *from* it as we have known it). As though the unconscious mind is moving ahead of our conscious mind, is perhaps at war with it.

That is how it was for Paul in the building up of a new idea at first unacceptable.

Like weighing sugar (or fixing powder for films, three ounces to a pint); the weights at one side, the growing pile, the sudden turn of the scales.

And so for Paul: the effect of Stephen's courage, of the spirit of the Christians he was persecuting; these made the gradual piling up. He gave himself no time to think, so busy was he harassing the Christians. Then he made a mistake. The long journey north to persecute the now scattered Christians meant time for reflection. The repressed admiration, the feeling for truth, the appeal of the gospel, burst through.

It happened in a thunderstorm, perhaps in a moment of fear. No recording camera would record all that happened. The flash of lightning, Yes; the thunder, Yes; but the words, No. What happened, happened in Paul's mind: the change was fundamental, but the sound-track would miss it.

This is a classic instance of a conversion, both gradual and sudden – gradual as when the sugar piled up on the scales, sudden as when the scales turned. It was a moment of vision; now he began to know what was happening to him.

We shall hear the bare story, just the few verses from the *Acts*; the rest later.

Reading

The reading is from the ninth chapter of the Acts of the Apostles:

Meanwhile Saul was still breathing murderous threats against the disciples of the Lord. He went to the High Priest and applied for letters to the synagogues at Damascus authorizing him to arrest anyone he found, men or women, who followed the new way, and bring them to Jerusalem. While he was still on the road and nearing Damascus, suddenly a light flashed from the sky all around him. He fell to the ground and heard a voice saying, 'Saul, Saul, why do you persecute me?' 'Tell me, Lord,' he said, 'who you are.' The voice answered, 'I am Jesus, whom you are persecuting. But get up and go into the city, and you will be told what you have to do.' Meanwhile the men who were travelling with him stood speechless; they heard the voice but could see no one. Saul got up from the ground, but when he opened his eyes he could not see; so they led him by the hand and brought him into Damascus. He was blind for three days, and took no food or drink.

Acts 9. 1–9 *NEB*

Let us pray

Lord God Almighty, whose eternal counsel ordereth all things, who hast ordained thy gracious purposes in the life of every man: Teach us to understand, and with glad heart to obey, thy will concerning us; knowing that without thee there can be at last no success, and with thee no failure; for thy Name's sake. Amen.

From Milner-White & Briggs, *Daily Prayer*, OUP, 1941

The Lord's Prayer

All   The grace of our Lord Jesus Christ,
                 and the love of God,
                 and the fellowship of the Holy Spirit,
              be with us all evermore. Amen.

Assembly 10 (2 of 4)
Once-, Twice-, & Oft-born

This assembly requires the use of a blackboard

Leader

You have all heard of exponential growth. The graph of it is like this – getting steeper as y increases.

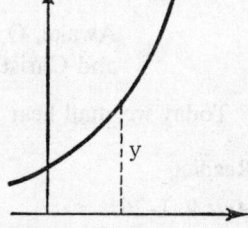

Yesterday we spoke of growth; growth of the early church, and in Paul.

We are all growing, physically, emotionally, intellectually, spiritually. Physical growth is the easiest to see and the easiest to measure; it often comes in spurts. There are discontinuities in the rates of other kinds of growth too; spiritual growth, for instance.

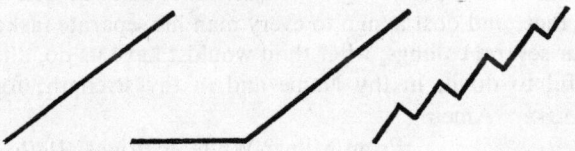

It can be steady, as in the first sketch, or it may involve one major change, or it may have many ups and downs. Psychologists sometimes speak of

    the once-born type   John was like this
    the twice-born type   Paul is an example
    the oft-born type   Peter was like this, and so are

most of us.

In this spiritual sense some are not born at all; they never get their feet off the ground. The graph is a horizontal line.

Paul was the twice-born sort . . . like Nicodemus who came to Jesus by night: 'You must be born from above', Jesus said (*John* 3. 7).

Yesterday we tried to understand the sudden change in his life, a conversion experience.

Two words are used: *arrested development*, when growth which might be expected does not take place. *Fixation*, when emotions tie you to a stage you should have out-grown.

It is often like this in religion. You remain immature because emotional fixation prevents growth. For Paul, the change was sudden. He had repressed the truth about himself, but it welled up from his own unconscious. No wonder, later, he could say:

> Awake, O sleeper, and rise from the dead,
> and Christ shall give you light (*Eph.* 5. 14).

Today we shall hear the whole story.

Reading

Acts 9. 1–26.

(This repeats the shorter passage heard yesterday.)

Let us pray

O God, who workest all things, who hast called us to be fellow-workers with thee, and dost assign to every man his separate task: Teach us, in our several callings, what thou wouldst have us do, and make us faithful to do it, in thy Name and in thy strength; for Jesus Christ's sake. Amen.

From Milner-White & Briggs, *Daily Prayer*,
OUP, 1941

All   The grace of our Lord Jesus Christ,
and the love of God,
and the fellowship of the Holy Spirit,
be with us all evermore. Amen.

Assembly 11 (3 of 4)
Peter's Vision

Leader

Christianity was at first a Jewish sect; Christians were followers of the new way – Jesus, the way, the truth, and the life (*John* 14. 6).

But could this good thing be limited to the Jews? What about the non-Jews? What of proselytes such as Cornelius, who, dissatisfied with pagan religions, turned to the God of Judaism? These questions vexed Peter.

Yesterday we saw that not all mental processes are logical; perhaps most are not. How did Peter's mind work? The various arguments were turning round in his head. Then, in a pictorial fashion, his immediate circumstances, the problem, and the answer, got all mixed up. But the answer was clear: 'God is no respecter of persons' – God does not have favourites.

Could this good news be for Jews only? Their law separated them, the law of clean and unclean, for instance: the camel, the badger, the hare, the pig, were not for Jews. But could this keep the good news from people?

He was at Joppa, a seaport town, the place Jonah sailed from. Jonah: the Old Testament story about God's universal love. Why, even the Ninevites were saved.

He was on the roof of the house waiting for his mid-day meal. Great sails, like sheets, were spread out in the harbour for repair.

He was hungry – perhaps the smell of food was rising.

All these things were mixed up in his half-dreaming, half-awake state. And the answer came; a kind of dialogue in his mind.

Reading

The reading is from the tenth chapter of the Acts of the Apostles.

About noon Peter went up on the roof to pray. He grew hungry and wanted something to eat. While they were getting it ready, he fell into a trance. He saw a rift in the sky, and a thing coming down that looked like a great sheet of sail-cloth. It was slung by the four corners, and was being lowered to the ground. In it he saw creatures of every kind, whatever walks or crawls or flies. Then there was a voice which said to him, 'Up, Peter, kill and eat.' But Peter said, 'No, Lord, no: I have never eaten anything profane or unclean.' The voice came again a second time: 'It is not for you to call profane what God counts clean.' This happened three times; and then the thing was taken up again into the sky.

While Peter was still puzzling over the meaning of the vision he had seen, the messengers of Cornelius had been asking the way to Simon's house, and now arrived at the entrance. They called out and asked if Simon Peter was lodging there. But Peter was thinking over the vision.

The story tells how Peter went to Caesarea to meet Cornelius, and what happened. It reports what Peter said, and includes these verses:

'I need not tell you that a Jew is forbidden by his religion to visit or associate with a man of another race; yet God has shown me clearly that I must not call any man profane or unclean. That is why I came here without demur when you sent for me.'

'I now see how true it is that God has no favourites, but that in every nation the man who is god-fearing and does what is right is acceptable to him.'

The story tells that the gift of the Holy Spirit came to all who were listening to Peter, even to Gentiles; and that they were baptized.

Acts 10. 9b–19a, 28, 29a, 34, 35 *NEB*

Let us pray

Almighty God, Father of all men, who hast given us by thy Son the good news of thy kingdom, grant that we may day by day have a fuller understanding of all that it means, and of the work we must do in it, that we may feel ourselves filled with a common purpose as fellow-workers with thee and each other, for the extension of that same kingdom, through Jesus Christ our Lord.

Source not known

The Lord's Prayer

All   The grace of our Lord Jesus Christ,
         and the love of God,
         and the fellowship of the Holy Spirit,
     be with us all evermore. Amen.

Assembly 12 (4 of 4)
No Favourites

Leader

Somehow the early Christians out-thought and out-lived the ancient world. The remarkable thing is that the band of first disciples, dispirited, let down as they thought at the crucifixion, nevertheless became a force to be reckoned with. The expansion was more than territorial; it was a vast expansion of thinking.

Yesterday's story is psychologically validated by twentieth-century thought. It is how, often, the truth dawns. For Peter 'God is no respecter of persons. In every nation the man who reverences him and does what is right is acceptable to him' (Phillips' translation). Or, as the New English Bible has it: 'I now see how true it is that God has no favourites.'

That is still hard for us to believe, hard to live by: witness, for instance, the question of colour. Later, Paul wrote to the Galatians: 'Gone is the distinction between Jew and Greek, slave and free man, male and female – you are all one in Christ Jesus' (*Gal.* 3. 28). They were the social distinctions of his day; our list would be different.

The lesson is one we still have to learn – that a man is what he does; that character, not race, matters. Peter's vision was authentic and its truth is not yet lived by. We prefer labels (Arab/Jew, Socialist/capitalist) to the reality of how men behave – what they are in themselves. 'God is no respecter of persons. In every nation the man who reverences him and does what is right is acceptable to him.'

Reading

The reading is part of the parable of the last judgment; it is from the twenty-fifth chapter of St Matthew:

'Lord, when was it that we saw you hungry and fed you, or thirsty and gave you drink, a stranger and took you home, or naked and clothed you? When did we see you ill or in prison, and come to visit you?' And the king will answer, 'I tell you this: anything you did for one of my brothers here, however humble, you did for me.'

Matt. 25. 37–40 *NEB*

Let us pray

Today we shall say two prayers, the first for ourselves and our own thinking, the second, for those in need.

Grant us, O Lord, the ability and the courage to see things as they are. May we look beyond the stereotype to the real person and the real situation. Widen our sympathy and compassion so that, understanding how others react, we may look beyond our private concerns to the common good, through Jesus Christ our Lord.

Almighty God, Father of all mankind, we think of the needs and despairs of countless lives broken by human enmity and indifference. Prosper all who seek to alleviate their suffering. Give wisdom to those who govern, and a great concern for human welfare to those in places of power. And hasten the day when love of their fellowmen will be the mark of all in authority, that thy kingdom may come on earth as it is in heaven. Amen.

The Lord's Prayer

All   The grace of our Lord Jesus Christ,
      and the love of God,
      and the fellowship of the Holy Spirit,
be with us all evermore.   Amen.

NOTES ON ASSEMBLIES 9–12

1. The days have gone when unexplained bible readings suffice for assemblies. The familiar stories must be approached with freshness and candour to make them acceptable; a psychological approach is often the most valuable. Colin Alves, in the British Council of Churches' report *Religion and the Secondary School* (SCM Press, 1968), says: 'Meaning always begins to take shape . . . *out of the experiences of the immediate present*, or *out of phenomena which are immediately apprehensible*,' and 'To present material from the past in isolation, however skilfully and vividly it is done, can never do more than make a momentary impression unless it is related to present experience and the continuing search for meaning' (p. 158).

2. The relation of biblical assemblies with the religious studies of the classroom is one for each school to work out. The function of assembly is not primarily exegetical or instructional, yet because each assembly is both an occasion and a collective experience, some things can be got over in assembly in a way not possible in the classroom. Much the same is true of music and the relation between a concert and class teaching.

3. One difficulty in this particular series concerns what to leave out. So much material is relevant; yet each assembly should not be too packed with ideas. I have found that what is presented here can, in fact, be taken: an earlier attempt included too much. Nevertheless, for Assembly 11, follow-up might include readings:

Lev. 11. 1–8 (*RSV*) for ritual uncleanness.
Jonah 1. 1–3; 4. 10–11 for references to Joppa.

The way in which St Luke repeats the telling of the stories shows the importance he attaches to these incidents.

4. The idea of a sudden conversion is made more acceptable by recognizing that it can be away from religion. One can become an atheist for righteousness' sake – when the only religion known does not satisfy the mind. Perhaps this explains much adolescent atheism: religious ideas have not grown with the rest of the psyche despite continued religious observances. Then, suddenly, the realization comes: 'Good gracious, I don't believe any of this!' – a sudden conversion. (Of course there may be other explanations: contra-suggestibility; or the desire to establish one's self-hood by standing out against what near adults value.) What is important is that students shall not assume that the religious person believes that *all* religion is good, or that *any* religion is better than none. Some forms of religion *should* drive men to unbelief.

5. The phrases 'once-born', 'twice-born', come from William James *The Varieties of Religious Experience* (Longmans, first edition 1902). Assembly 10 says that most of us, like Peter, are in the oft-born category. We have many ups and downs. It is to be hoped that the ups exceed the downs. A follow-up exercise could be to trace the story of Peter in the gospels, and his misunderstandings, until he became a pillar of the early church as Acts portrays.

III *Working Together*

EDWIN COX, in *Sixth Form Religion* (SCM Press, 1967), analyzes students' attitudes, and comments on what he describes as 'perhaps the biggest theological problem of our age, i.e. the relation of a spiritual God to an apparently self-contained creation capable of empirical understanding' (p. 41). 'It would seem,' he says, 'that there are two areas in which (Sixth Formers') thinking operates, which are to some extent mutually exclusive. Some tend to think mainly in one area, others in the other area, but the majority vacillate between the two. These areas are roughly . . . factual statements and value judgments . . . two types of thought . . . empirical thinking and teleological thinking.' He continues, 'Empirical thinking, with its greater communicability and its susceptibility to verification, seems the less hazardous exercise' (p. 174).

This, of course, is the stuff of both General Studies and Religious Studies, and both the Christian and the humanist have a part to play. Forty years ago A. N. Whitehead in *Science and the Modern World* wrote of the 'conflict' between science and religion, and confidently asserted that 'the clash is a sign that there are wider truths and finer perspectives within which a reconciliation of a deeper religion and a more subtle science will be found'. He made the point 'that religion is the expression of one type of fundamental experiences of mankind; that religious thought develops into an increasing accuracy of expression, disengaged from adventitious imagery: that the interaction between religion and science is one great factor in promoting this development'. It is still necessary, as we have seen, to do the disengaging and to explain this interaction.

Some assemblies will quite properly be concerned with these issues. It is therefore important to ensure that the right questions are asked. Right answers *cannot* be given. 'Right answers' have a way of being wrong answers for many; 'right answers' imply that discussion is closed, the goal is reached. There is, of course, no virtue in indecision; virtue lies in that kind of commitment to truth which leaves the mind open to explore. Men have to live with unresolved problems in other spheres, in science and in economics, for instance. Sides may be taken on both emotional and logical grounds; what matters is that thinking should continue. There are unresolved problems, tensions, too, in religion; often they are at growing points, and they have their concomitant growing pains.

The former Bishop of Woolwich, Dr J. A. T. Robinson, expresses the 'biggest theological problem' differently. In *Exploration into God* (SCM Press, 1967), after speaking of fashions in theology and of the several major concerns of recent decades, he says that 'now we are agitated, most deeply of all, by a thorough-going reappraisal of the doctrine of *God*' (p. 29). But this time there is a difference – the dialogue is not within the Church, demanding the attention of the theologically trained only; it has burst out beyond the bounds of institutional religion to speak to and for a far wider audience. Now, 'God' is news.

Here, too, Christian and humanist can explore together. It is fortunate for education that Dr Robinson, in *Exploration into God*, has made so readily available the way in which radical Christian thinking is progressing; it makes theology once more a central issue.

'You lean over backwards to meet the unbeliever', was the mild rebuke of a sound and sympathetic churchman when I explained how I approached the conducting of assembly. Dr Robinson puts it differently: 'What Christians and humanists have in common is a shared concern, commitment, intention, and this is frequently more significant than how they articulate it or define it' (p. 82). His own articulation shuns 'a Supreme Being type of theology', but has room for 'The primal experience of being human is to find oneself held in a relationship of sustaining, claiming love' (p. 133). Nevertheless articulation remains difficult, for words are poor things.

Somehow, through the short sonnet-style of assemblies, the excitement of the current dialogue should be conveyed. And if students see where the headmaster stands, they should know that there is no snub if they differ; other leaders of assembly may differ too. But despite differences, despite the various starting points, all can embrace ideals. An aim of education is to make people capable of sincerity: one way may be through the agnosticism of faith.

And if the headmaster himself is a humanist, what then? I hope he will be among those who share the 'concern, commitment, intention' of which Dr Robinson speaks. The job itself takes a man in this direction. Schoolmastering, conscientiously undertaken, soon becomes a way of life, and concern for pupils a challenge to meet the human situation at all levels; headmastering hastens this evolution. I should hope that the humanist headmaster will be ready to work with senior colleagues who are Christians and who are willing to co-operate in leading assembly, provided that, along with him, they have discovered that 'it is less a matter of finding than of seeking, or, one might say, of finding that attitude which consists in seeking'.*
They are as likely to be on the science side of his staff as on the arts side. Much better for him to share the leading of assemblies than to adopt a conformist position insincerely. In fact, for a headmaster to be present when a colleague is using Christian phraseology not within his compass, though he himself expresses aspirations in other terms is itself, for pupils, an education in human understanding. What should always be avoided is the arrogance, whether in the Christian or in the humanist, which excludes all other answers.

Among the seven assemblies that follow, Assembly 16 is a remarkable voice from the eighteenth century. I am indebted to Mr M. J. Rayner, who, in his first post at Huddersfield New College, is now in charge of General Studies, for drafting Assemblies 17–19. He has avoided conventional religious language, yet touched on some of the determinants of psychological growth. These three assemblies are incomplete; they have been left at a middle stage of drafting in order to indicate some of the difficulties which a non-preacher meets. (See, also, the notes that follow them.)

* Paul Tournier in *A Doctor's Casebook in the Light of the Bible*, SCM Press, 1954, p. 34.

One Remove from Reality: Personal Relations

Leader

I wonder whether any of you, thinking of your childhood, have been unable to separate memory of events from memory of the recounting of events? I remember such an occasion.

I must have been five or six at the time. We were on a steamer which ran aground near Filey Brigg. There was no real danger except fog. The Filey lifeboat picked up the passengers, and the Filey sands were full of people with hot drinks and food for the ship-wrecked.

The story was told again and again in the family circle, and I do not know whether I remember the event or only the account, frequently told, of the event – the reality, or the words telling of it. It is as though words describing an experience separate us from the experience.

A similar ambiguity sometimes marks our relations with people. An employer thinking of an employee, a teacher thinking of a pupil, a headmaster thinking of a member of his staff – each may see not a person, but a label. For me the label might have had three words on it: mathematics, religious education, photography. I am never seen as a person to get to know, but as someone who might be referred to on any of these three matters. The person is not seen, only the label.

You may, yourself, sometimes feel that you are not known as a person; you are thought of solely as a function, perhaps to fit into a prescribed niche. But you *are* a person, and you feel like revolt when this is not recognized.

Does this often happen? In other things too? – the reality not known, but only the words telling of it or purporting to tell of it.

The man who holds conventional views about music, but who has no experience of the spiritual quickening which music affords, is like that. He does not know the real thing, only the accepted, the received attitude towards it.

The man who groups all Scots or all West Indians or all Pakistanis under a single label, and then never sees the individual person as a person, but sees only the category, is like that. And yet a single genuine personal contact could reveal real flesh and blood and, maybe, dissolve prejudice.

One of the purposes of education is to help us to know for ourselves so that we cease to be content with second-hand opinion. Too often we are one remove from reality. To escape this, we *must* escape it first at some one point, else we shall never become capable of sincerity. To be sincere at one point is the beginning of being sincere throughout. Intellectual sincerity has to be won; and, even more, emotional sincerity has to be won. Then we shall by-pass the label, the category, the conventional, and know for ourselves.

We shall not say a prayer today; instead we shall hear part of Psalm 139 in the Knox translation, and then one verse of a nineteenth-century hymn. You could, of course, make either into a meditation or a prayer. But first a quotation from Aldous Huxley. In a chapter headed 'Truth' in his book *The Perennial Philosophy*, after speaking of 'truth' as 'fact', he writes: 'But this is clearly not the meaning of the word in such a phrase as "worshipping God in spirit and in truth". Here, it is obvious, "truth" signifies direct apprehension of spiritual Fact, as opposed to second-hand knowledge *about* Reality, formulated in sentences and accepted on authority or because an argument from previously granted postulates was logically convincing.' And this fits in with our thinking this morning.

Reading

LORD, I lie open to thy scrutiny; thou knowest me.
Where can I go, then, to take refuge from thy spirit, to hide
    from thy view? If I should climb up to heaven, thou art
    there; if I sink down to the world beneath, thou art
    present still. If I could wing my way eastwards, or find
    a dwelling beyond the western sea, still would I find
    thee beckoning to me, thy right hand upholding me. Or
    perhaps I would think to bury myself in darkness; night
    should surround me, friendlier than day; but no, darkness
    is no hiding-place from thee, with thee the night shines
    clear as day itself; light and dark are one.
Author, thou, of my inmost being, didst thou not form me in
    my mother's womb? I praise thee for my wondrous fashioning,
    for all the wonders of thy creation.

A riddle, O my God, thy dealings with me, so vast their scope!
 As well count the sand, as try to fathom them; and, were
 that skill mine, thy own being still confronts me.
Ps. 139. 1, 7–14, 17, 18 *Knox*

Solo Voice

> Thou must be true thyself,
> If thou the truth wouldst teach;
> Thy soul must overflow, if thou
> Another's soul wouldst reach:
> It needs the overflow of heart
> To give the lips full speech.

Horatius Bonar; Tune: *Loyalty*

Recording

The 2½-minute chorale prelude *Alle Menschen müssen sterben* from the record of Bach's organ music SAWT 9444-B (side 2, band 7) would be suitable.

One Remove from Reality: Physical Sciences

Leader

There are many ways of knowing; many kinds of knowledge. Three are obvious at a cursory glance:

> We know *that* Leeds is sixteen miles from Huddersfield;
> We know *how* to prove Pythagoras's theorem;
> We *know* John Smith, he's a good friend of ours.

Knowing *that*, knowing *how*, *knowing* John, involve us in different ways.

Ever since C. P. Snow delivered his famous lecture *The Two Cultures* the differences between the sciences and the humanities have been recognized, though the idea of a Snow-line (as it has been called) is quite old. Hear a passage by A. S. Eddington, one of the first of the great astronomers who have been able to write popularly about cosmologies. His book *The Nature of the Physical World* (CUP, 1928), now a classic, was written forty years ago.

Reading

One of the greatest changes in Physics between the nineteenth century and the present day (that is, the nineteen-twenties) has been the change in our ideal of scientific explanation. It was the boast of the Victorian physicist that he would not claim to understand a thing until he could make a model of it; and by a model he meant something constructed of levers, geared wheels, squirts, or other appliances familiar to an engineer. Nature in building the universe was supposed to be dependent on just the same kind of resources as any human mechanic; and when the physicist sought an explanation of phenomena his ear was straining to catch the hum of machinery. The man who could make gravitation out of cog-wheels would have been a hero in the Victorian age.

Nowadays we do not encourage the engineer to build the world for us out of his material, but we turn to the mathematician to build it out of his material. Doubtless the mathematician is a loftier being than the engineer, but perhaps even he ought not to be entrusted with the Creation unreservedly. We are dealing in physics with a symbolic world, and we can scarcely avoid employing the mathematician who is the professional wielder of symbols.

(from Chapter X)

Leader

What does Eddington mean by 'a symbolic world'? We can say that the scientist's explanation is a kind of map; it portrays what it is intended to convey, but it is not the reality. It has its own internal consistency as a good map has, but not even the best Ordnance map *is* the countryside. Indeed just as there are many projections in map-making, so there are different theories – different mathematical models – in the physical sciences. Even a temporary sketch-map may be of use.

To ask 'Does an electron exist?' is the wrong kind of question. The right question is 'Does the *idea* of an electron help us to understand how things behave? Does it make part of a consistent and useful map?'

And always there is more than symbolic knowledge, for other ways of apprehension are also necessary if we are to see life whole. Eddington speaks of symbolic knowledge and intimate knowledge – but this we shall follow up tomorrow. It is parallel, in some ways, to Snow's two cultures.

Let us pray

Lord, we thank you for the fascination of our own particular line of study, and we thank you also for the great variety of ways in which men can look at your world and map it.

Save us from thinking that we can, ourselves, encompass all the truth; save us from regarding what others discover by different methods with disdain, or of less importance, just because what they have found does not fit into our map.

Above all, help us to be right in what we value; help us to value mind more than matter, people more than things, and a personal relatedness more than a codified system, so that we become better inhabitants of your many-faceted world. Amen.

One Remove from Reality: Theology

Leader

Professor A. S. Eddington of Cambridge was a mathematical astronomer; he was also a Quaker. I think this will emerge from today's reading from his book *The Nature of the Physical World* (CUP, 1928). The paragraph (from Chapter XV) is headed *Symbolic Knowledge and Intimate Knowledge*.

First Reading

We have two kinds of knowledge which I call symbolic knowledge and intimate knowledge. I do not know whether it would be correct to say that reasoning is only applicable to symbolic knowledge, but the more customary forms of reasoning have been developed for symbolic knowledge only. The intimate knowledge will not submit to codification and analysis; or, rather, when we attempt to analyze it the intimacy is lost and it is replaced by symbolism.

For an illustration let us consider Humour. I suppose that humour can be analyzed to some extent and the essential ingredients of the different kinds of wit classified. Suppose that we are offered an alleged joke. We submit it to scientific analysis as we would a chemical salt of doubtful nature, and perhaps after careful consideration of all its aspects we are able to confirm that it really and truly is a joke. Logically, I suppose, our next procedure would be to laugh. But it may certainly be predicted that as the result of this scrutiny we shall have lost all inclination we may ever have had to laugh at it. It simply does not do to expose the inner workings of a joke. The classification concerns a symbolic knowledge of humour which preserves all the characteristics of a joke except its laughableness. The real appreciation must come spontaneously, not introspectively. I think this is a not unfair analogy for our mystical feeling for nature, and I would venture even to apply it to our mystical experience of God. There are some to whom the sense of a divine presence irradiating the soul is one of the most obvious things of experience. In their view a man without this sense is to be regarded as we regard a man without a sense of humour. The absence is a kind of mental deficiency. We may try to analyze the experience as we analyze humour, and construct a theology, or it may be an atheistic philosophy, which shall put into scientific form what is to be inferred about it. But let us not forget that the theology is symbolic knowledge whereas the experience is intimate knowledge. And as laughter cannot be compelled by the scientific exposition of the structure of a joke, so a philosophic discussion of the attributes of God (or an impersonal substitute) is likely to miss the intimate response of the spirit which is the central point of the religious experience.

Leader

And so Eddington says that as soon as we try to communicate immediate experience the words we use themselves become a barrier and take us one remove from reality. And yet communication is necessary for us, whether in words, themselves symbols, or in the acted symbols of the liturgy. There is always the danger of knowledge being formal; whether of people, using labels and categories, or of physics, thinking symbolic knowledge is all, or of religion, being content with right doctrine. Symbolic knowledge must be supplemented with intimate knowledge.

There is a scriptural reading which ties up with this, a favourite one of Eddington's. It is about Elijah, feeling flat after the excitement of Mount Carmel, and about the voice of the Lord, not in the wonders of nature, but in 'the still small voice' – 'the whisper of a gentle breeze' as one translator has it.

Second Reading

Elijah came to a cave and lodged there; and behold, the word of the Lord came to him, and he said to him, 'What are you doing here, Elijah?' He said, 'I have been very jealous for the Lord, the God of hosts; for the people of Israel have forsaken thy covenant, thrown down thy altars, and slain thy prophets with the sword; and I, even I only, am left; and they seek my life, to take it away.' And he said, 'Go forth, and stand upon the mount before the Lord.' And behold, the Lord passed by, and a great and strong wind rent the mountains, and broke in pieces the rocks before the Lord, but the Lord was not in the wind; and after the wind an earthquake, but the Lord was not in the earthquake; and after the earthquake a fire, but the Lord was not in the fire; and after the fire a still small voice.

And when Elijah heard it, he wrapped his face in his mantle and went out and stood at the entrance of the cave. And behold there came a voice to him, and said, 'What are you doing here, Elijah?'

I Kings 19. 9–13 *RSV*

Let us pray

Grant, O Lord, that when we fail to see thee in the impersonality of pure science, or in the pragmatism of technology, or in the interpretations of social science, or in any formal or symbolic knowledge, we may yet discover thee in the still small voice, in the light which lighteth every man, and in the word made flesh. Amen.

All The grace of our Lord Jesus Christ,
and the love of God,
and the fellowship of the Holy Spirit,
be with us all evermore. Amen.

NOTES ON ASSEMBLIES 13-15

1. These assemblies are full of material belonging to General Studies; they could well be used when C. P. Snow's *The Two Cultures and the Scientific Revolution* (CUP, 1959) is being discussed. John Habgood's *Religion and Science* (Mills & Boon, 1964) will also be found useful, as well as the terms 'casual', 'functional', 'personal' in regard to human relationships (see p. 123 in *Exploration into God*), and 'public' and 'private' in regard to knowledge.

2. Some consideration of Edwin Cox's dilemma about teleology and science will be found in A. R. Bielby's *Sixth Form Worship*, (SCM Press, 1968) Assemblies 31–33.

3. The different styles of 'prayer' used here have point, if only to gain flexibility. A minor consideration is that students should feel no uncertainty about when the religious part of assembly has ended. When there is no formal prayer and *amen* I think that the use of carefully chosen music as an integral part of assembly *before* announcements and dismissal is of value. Another consideration involves pronouns. In formal prayer the use of 'you' instead of 'thou' is becoming more accepted in churches and should be equally acceptable in assembly, but the traditional 'thou' should be used when versions of the bible which use 'thou' are included.

Assembly 16
A Catholic Spirit

Leader

Men differ in opinion; must they then quarrel? They embrace different loyalties; must they then hate each other?

Or is argument, conflict of ideas, possible at one level and, at another, a deep concern for the common good, and with it mutual love?

John Wesley thought so. We shall hear parts of a sermon, published as one of 53 in 1771. He chose as starting point a brief conversation reported in the bible:

'Is thine heart right, as my heart is with thy heart?'
'It is.'
'If it be, give me thine hand.'

II *Kings* 10. 15

First Reading

Although a difference in opinions or modes of worship may prevent an entire external union, yet need it prevent our union in affection? Though we cannot think alike, may we not love alike? May we not be of one heart, though we are not of one opinion? Without all doubt, we may.

Leader

As we hear further extracts, transfer the argument to other spheres where men differ. Wesley speaks of what he calls 'invincible ignorance', even 'invincible prejudice', in others; can he, or any man, be sure that he is himself in no respect mistaken?

Second Reading

Every wise man will allow others the same liberty of thinking which he desires they should allow him; and will no more insist on their embracing his opinions, than he would have them insist on his embracing theirs. He bears with those who differ from him, and only asks him with whom he desires to unite in love that single question, 'Is thy heart right, as my heart is with thy heart?'

. . . .

I dare not presume to impose my mode of worship on any other.

I believe it is truly primitive and apostolic: but my belief is no rule for another. I ask not, therefore, of him with whom I would unite in love, Are you of my church? or my congregation? Do you receive the same form of Church government, and allow the same Church officers, with me? Do you join in the same form of prayer wherein I worship God? I inquire not, Do you receive the supper of the Lord in the same posture and manner that I do? nor whether, in the administration of baptism, you agree with me in admitting sureties for the baptized; in the manner of administering it; or the age of those to whom it should be administered. Nay, I ask not of you, (as clear as I am in my own mind,) whether you allow baptism and the Lord's supper at all. Let all these things stand by: we will talk of them, if need be, at a more convenient season; my only question at present is this, 'Is thine heart right, as my heart is with thy heart?'
. . . .
'If it be, give me thy hand.' I do not mean, 'Be of my opinion.' You need not: I do not expect it or desire it. Neither do I mean, '*I* will be of your opinion.' I cannot: it does not depend on my choice: I can no more think, than I can see or hear, as I will. Keep you your opinion; I mine; and that as steadily as ever. You need not even endeavour to come over to me, or bring me over to you. I do not desire you to dispute those points, or to hear or speak one word concerning them. Let all opinions alone on one side and the other: only 'give me thine hand'.

I do not mean, 'Embrace my modes of worship'; or, 'I will embrace yours.' This also is a thing which does not depend either on your choice or mine. We must both act as each is fully persuaded in his own mind. Hold fast that which you believe is most acceptable to God, and I will do the same. . . . I believe infants ought to be baptized; and that this may be done either by dipping or sprinkling. If you are otherwise persuaded, be so still, and follow your own persuasion. It appears to me, that forms of prayer are of excellent use, particularly in the great congregation. If you judge extemporary prayer to be of more use, act suitable to your own judgment. . . . Let all these smaller points stand aside. Let them never come into sight. 'If thine heart is as my heart,' if thou lovest God and all mankind, I ask no more: 'give me thine hand.'

Leader

The sermon is a long one, closely reasoned, and most generous in spirit. But does union in love mean forgetting differences? Is Wesley saying, 'Let us be woolly in order to be matey?' Never!

Third Reading

First, a catholic spirit is not *speculative* latitudinarianism. It is not an indifference to all opinions: this is the spawn of hell, not the offspring of heaven. This unsettledness of thought, this being 'driven to and fro, and tossed about with every wind of doctrine', is a great curse, not a blessing; an irreconcilable enemy, not a friend, to true catholicism. A man of a truly catholic spirit has not now his religion to seek. He is fixed as the sun in his judgment concerning the main branches of Christian doctrine. . . . He does not halt between two opinions, nor vainly endeavour to blend them into one. Observe this, you who know not what spirit ye are of: who call yourselves men of a catholic spirit, only because you are of a muddy understanding; because your mind is all in a mist; because you have no settled, consistent principles, but are for jumbling all opinions together. Be convinced, that you have quite missed your way; you know not where you are. . . .

Secondly, a catholic spirit is not any kind of *practical* latitudinarianism. It is not indifference as to public worship, or as to the outward manner of performing it. . . .

But while he is steadily fixed in his religious principles, in what he believes to be the truth as it is in Jesus; while he firmly adheres to that worship of God, which he judges to be most acceptable in his sight; . . . his heart is enlarged to all mankind, those he knows and those he does not; he embraces with strong and cordial affection neighbours and strangers, friends and enemies. This is catholic or universal love. And he that has this is of a catholic spirit.

Let us pray

Fill our hearts, O Lord, with love for thee and for one another. Help us each to know clearly where he stands. In our dealings save us from meanness and from imputing unworthy motives. Let our minds be ready always to believe good rather than evil of one another. Forgive our past failures, and enable us each day to gain a surer mastery of ourselves and a firmer hold on all that is good.

May our hearts be right with others, that we may be ready to respond, 'Give me thine hand.' Amen.

Assembly 17 (1 of 3; incomplete)
A Clear View: Describing People

Leader

Whatever our religious views, we are faced with the task of co-operating with our fellow men in this life. There is no easy method of doing this successfully, as conflicts show. But at least we can start with a clear view of other people, without which our efforts and contacts will fail. This and the following two assemblies touch on three aspects of gaining a clear view. Today's aspect may be called: Describing People.

Most of the words we use are general, that is, they lump together similar things. The word 'dog' collects all those animals which have the characteristics of dogs. Such general words are very useful, indeed, indispensable to a language. Unfortunately, they are sometimes too coarse and clumsy, and cover up distinctions which we ought to make. Macbeth makes this point when replying to the protest of one of the murderers, 'We are men, my liege.'

First Reading

> Ay, in the catalogue ye go for men;
> As hounds and greyhounds, mongrels, spaniels, curs,
> Shoughs, water-rugs and demi-wolves, are clept
> All by the name of dogs: the valued file
> Distinguishes the swift, the slow, the subtle,
> The housekeeper, the hunter, every one
> According to the gift which bounteous nature
> Hath in him closed, whereby he does receive
> Particular addition, from the bill
> That writes them all alike: and so of men.
>
> *Macbeth*, Act III, Scene i

Leader

When we are describing humans, the temptation is there to lump them together unjustifiably, denying their individuality. If we do this we cut ourselves off from the truth about them. Words like

'Conservative', 'Labour', 'Liberal', 'Communist', 'Fascist', 'Middle-class', 'The Young', 'Old People', 'The Establishment', 'intellectuals', and so on, are used to group qualities, and they mislead us if they make us think that because one man, for example, votes Labour he has other qualities or opinions in common with other Labour voters. He may have or he may not.

All too often we classify others in order to dismiss them as unworthy of further consideration, making life easier for us, perhaps allowing us to be escapist. The individual has been placed in a packing case with other individuals and can now be shipped out of our view.

It is when we are at the receiving end of such treatment that we protest about labelling. 'But I'm not the same as other Englishmen', you protest, when a Frenchman insists that all Englishmen are deceitful; or, 'I may live in a suburb but that doesn't mean that I like plastic gnomes in my garden', you retort to the facile categorist of suburban behaviour. We rightly resent being labelled and relegated. 'One star differeth from another star in glory', as the New Testament says, or, put another way by W. S. Gilbert when he wanted to prevent wholesale dismissal of aristocracy as corrupt and worthless compared with the simple virtues of the poor:

> Hearts just as pure and fair
> May beat in Belgrave Square
> As in the lowly air
> Of Seven Dials.

(Iolanthe)

To describe others sweepingly will never help us to see them as they really are. Just as a fixed-lens camera will give a picture which is sometimes fuzzy and so no longer accurate because it cannot adjust to differences in the world, so inflexible application of words to people will distort the truth.

Two short readings may illustrate the point further. First, a historian writing about the use of the words *middle class* in nineteenth-century politics:

Second Reading

... it should become the custom when anyone shows a tendency to talk about the middle class, to make him answer this simple but very difficult question – 'Who precisely were the middle class?' Presumably they were all the people who at any given moment came in income, or in social estimation, between the nobility and landed gentry on the one hand and the manual labourers on a weekly or daily wage on the other. If so, the bracket is a wide one. On this calculation a merchant prince in Liverpool would be middle class or a banker in the City and at the same time a linen draper in Exeter would be middle class and so would be those cheeky, shabby clerks you so often meet in Dickens. The range of income must have been very great, and the variety in ways of life almost beyond calculation, particularly if you include not only the town but the countryside, the tenant farmers, the corn merchants, the millers, in fact all that society which George Eliot knew so well.

From G. Kitson Clark, *The Making of Victorian England*, Methuen, 1962

Leader

Secondly, some words from *A Song of Patriotic Prejudice* by Michael Flanders which was sung with Donald Swann who wrote the music in *At the Drop of Another Hat*. The opinions expressed are satiric and not their own!

> The Scotsman is mean as we're all well aware,
> And bony and blotchy and covered with hair.
> He eats salty porridge, he works all the day,
> And he hasn't got Bishops to show him the way.
>
> The Irishman now our contempt is beneath.
> He sleeps in his boots and he lies in his teeth.
> He blows up policemen, or so I have heard,
> And blames it on Cromwell and William the Third.
>
> The Welshman's dishonest: he cheats when he can,
> And little and dark, more like monkey than man.
> He works underground with a lamp in his hat,
> And sings far too loud, far too often, and flat.
>
> The English are moral, the English are good,
> And clever and modest and misunderstood.

From *A Song of Patriotic Prejudice* by Michael Flanders with music by Donald Swann as sung by them in *At the Drop of Another Hat*, Parlophone PCS 3052.

Assembly 18 (2 of 3; incomplete)

A Clear View: Ascribing Motives

Leader

Yesterday we saw that to describe people in categories is to distort the truth about the individual. Today, we consider the second of our three aspects of gaining a clear view.

In dealing with other people we need to know them as they really are. For this we often need to find out the reasons why a person took the action he did. Only then can we know what to expect from them. Much of our detection work consists in finding the other person's motives. Now this is a difficult task because motives are not open to inspection but are inferred from behaviour. The easiest course – and the most stupid and unjust – is to have a short-list of motives which we invoke over and over again to do our explaining. The problem is that the short-list is often not long enough.

Everyone must have experienced frustration and anger when his motives have been misinterpreted. In schools some teachers are particularly miserly with their short-list: that pupil's talking is a piece of deliberate misbehaviour, another's poor performance is because he isn't working. No alternatives are admitted. Perhaps this example is an exaggeration, but it makes the point clear.

The penalties of an error in finding a person's reasons for action can be trivial, a matter merely of irritation, or, at the other end of the scale, tragic. Anyone who has read *Othello* will be aware of the consequences of misinterpreting motives. Othello is misled by Iago and misinterprets his wife's actions, not admitting to himself any other explanation than her infidelity. As a result he kills her.

In daily life such misinterpretations can lose friendships, cause industrial strife, provoke wars. Whatever it does, it makes us see others less clearly. The man who walks past the flag-seller may be deemed hard-hearted and mean. Consider, though, some of the other possibilities: he may not have seen the flag-seller, he may be in a temporary bad mood and feel ungenerous, he may have bought a flag and lost it, he may have no money or small change on him, he may object in principle to the necessity for charities to have to beg in a Welfare State, he may be in a hurry, he may contribute to a charity already and think that is enough, or he may object to having his conscience twisted by having a collection tin shaken under his nose. If we grant all these as possibilities, it is surely slick and precipitate to label him as hard-hearted and mean and dismiss him without consideration. Automatic interpretation blinds us to the real reasons others have for their actions and leads to friction.

A reading which illustrates the misinterpretations of motives is taken from James Joyce's *A Portrait of the Artist as a Young Man* (Jonathan Cape, 1916). Stephen Dedalus, a pupil at school, has had his glasses broken through no fault of his own. The prefect of studies, a senior master, comes into the class and finds Stephen not working.

Reading

– You, boy, who are you?
  Stephen's heart jumped suddenly.
– Dedalus, sir.
– Why are you not writing like the others?
– I . . , my . . .
  He could not speak with fright.
– Why is he not writing, Father Arnall?
– He broke his glasses, said Father Arnall, and I exempted him from work.
– Broke? What is this I hear? What is this your name is! said the prefect of studies.
– Dedalus, sir.
– Out here, Dedalus. Lazy little schemer. I see schemer in your face. Where did you break your glasses?
  Stephen stumbled into the middle of the class, blinded by fear and haste.
– Where did you break your glasses? repeated the prefect of studies.
– The cinderpath, sir.
– Hoho! The cinderpath! cried the prefect of studies. I know that trick.
  Stephen lifted his eyes in wonder and saw for a moment Father Dolan's whitegrey not young face, his baldy whitegrey head with fluff

at the sides of it, the steel rims of his spectacles and his nocoloured eyes looking through the glasses. Why did he say he knew that trick?
– Lazy idle little loafer! cried the prefect of studies. Broke my glasses! An old schoolboy trick! Out with your hands this moment!

(from page 51)

Assembly 19 (3 of 3; incomplete)
A Clear View: Removing Scales

Leader

The third aspect of our gaining a clear view is not as easy to define as the other two. It can best be called 'losing the scales from your eyes'. We see people in their everyday activities, sometimes accurately, sometimes erroneously, yet even if we see the individual actions of a person clearly we do not always see the person himself. His actions, taken together, do not make a pattern for us. However, there are occasions when suddenly all the individual facts add up to something more, a pattern appears which changes the way we see the person. We feel that before this revelation we were blind. Now we see.

There is a story, invented by a philosopher, of a woman who tries on a new hat and finds it difficult to decide whether it suits her or not. A friend resolves the difficulty by declaring that the hat is the Taj Mahal. Suddenly the woman knows the hat isn't for her – she suddenly recognizes what has been there all the time. The hat hasn't changed in any way. What has changed is the way the facts are seen. With people, the facts are there, but how they add up and what the total is is not always realized.

Many novelists portray the stages by which characters come to see other people as they really are, anew and correctly. In Jane Austen's *Northanger Abbey* the heroine, Catherine Morland, in her friendship with Isabella Thorpe, goes through these stages. She fails to see what Isabella adds up to – a frivolous, snobbish, grasping, mercenary, and hypocritical woman. The reader sees this early on, but it is not until Isabella writes a letter to Catherine, near the end of the book, that the scales fall from Catherine's eyes. Isabella is engaged to Catherine's brother but has been flirting with a Captain Tilney.

Reading

From *Northanger Abbey*, Chapter XXVII: the letter, and the lines following it telling of Catherine's reaction, to '... her demands impudent'.

NOTES ON ASSEMBLIES 17-19

1. *Difficulties of composition*

Mr Rayner, when he had got as far with these assemblies as is set out here, commented on the task:

'The exercise of drafting assemblies is not an easy one; it seems to demand different skills and a different approach from ordinary teaching. I found three main difficulties:

The first was in deciding on material. The purpose is not just exposition; I felt I had to "advise" or "influence" the students in a way that I am not conscious of in my ordinary work. Not being a preacher, or wanting to be one, I was entering unfamiliar territory.

The second was style. Should the preacher be declamatory? Is his job to give a spiritual pep-talk? Or to persuade to some viewpoint, or to some action? Illustrations, too, came hard. Does the preacher regard everything he sees or reads as source-material?

And thirdly, how should an assembly be rounded off if the conventional ending, the prayer, is to be avoided? Even with prayers, and I am willing to compose them, I would not find it easy.'

2. *Requirements*

I agree with Mr Rayner that the usual schoolmasterly skills do not necessarily equip a man for taking assembly. A 'churchy' style is to be avoided, but some kinds of church work, and especially local-preacher training, can be a help. It is necessary to be clear about what one is doing, and about its importance. One should know how students (or children) think and react. *Time* is required (I reckoned an hour an evening, on the average), and, I think, the humility and sincerity implied in the substance of the next paragraph.

3. *What the leader of assembly stands for*

Above all, in assembly, the leader has a representative job. He does not speak *for* himself; behind his words is a 'thus saith the Lord' element. He speaks *to* himself as well as to the students. There is an Absolute to encounter, whether personalized as 'God', or not. And because he is aware of this, the leader of assembly can be strong in faith and humble before truth at the same time. He speaks 'from faith to faith', and, in so doing, grows in the job.

4. *The essential ingredient*

It is hard to see that assembly can have any religious value without this recognition; and it is hard to see that an education is adequate which ignores its possibility.

IV *Participation*

THE first three chapters of this book have presented the need for and the possibility of the humanist and the Christian working together in the daily act of worship. True, the churchman may feel that school worship as described here is a far cry from what goes on in churches, so that it scarcely provides an introduction to it. The humanist also may have qualms: is he not yielding something vital by accepting word-forms which imply the personalizing of his spiritual awareness, even though, when conducting assembly himself, he does not use them? Yet the two *can* work together, their common educational purpose and the needs of pupils over-riding differences. Not all religious people are ready to do this, however; nor all humanists. Nor, indeed, is the leading of assembly everybody's job, however sympathetic they may be to its aims. I have tried, both in the text, and in the illustrative assemblies, to indicate attitudes which make for such co-operation; it is enriching for those who share in the work, and unifying in its influence on the school. It requires that the humanist and the believer share the humility that enables each to accept for himself the aphorism 'Most thoughtful men are right in what they affirm and wrong in what they deny'. The general tenor of assemblies, nevertheless, remains Christian.

There are many reasons for this: one is that our traditions are Christian, so that most of the language and symbols of the inner life derive from Christianity. Another is that an atheist (or a humanist) in a Christian context is a different kind of atheist (or a humanist) from one in a non-Christian context. It is not merely that many of them are lapsed Christians, or rebels against conventional forms of Christianity, but that Christian standards permeate our common life and are taken over by all men of goodwill. In this sense Christianity is part of our culture and it is proper that schools should seek to transmit this, and also to define its source. The traditional Christian may wryly add 'And this is because Christianity is true, so why not say so?'; the radical starts differently: today's approach must be empiric; the Christian revelation will only be seen to be true if it provides answers to human needs and meets the human situation at its deepest. First we must learn what it is to be a *man*. This is a task which the humanist and Christian can share.

This non-prescriptive attitude is in keeping with current educational trends and comprises part of the current dilemma about the nature of authority. As regards school assemblies, it means that these cannot be run from above; student participation is essential.

The assemblies set out in Chapters I–III assume the readiness of both staff and students to co-operate – staff, in assembly sequences which are a kind of team-teaching; students, in prepared reading and singing. But co-operation is not only in the act of worship itself; there is assumed also a readiness to follow up the themes of assembly in subsequent discussion.

In this chapter we look at other forms of participation under the headings:

A *Individual participation* (p. 74)
B *Group participation* (p. 82)
C *Audience participation* (p. 95)
D *Behind-the-scenes participation* (p. 105)

and illustrate by further examples. (It will be evident that throughout this book the worked-out assemblies do not provide a scheme to be followed, nor do they make a balanced whole. They are included both to show what is possible and to develop further the ideas of the text.)

A · Individual Participation

The establishing of a format which encouraged individual participation was, at Huddersfield New College, partly fortuitous, partly planned. The Physical Education department preferred Thursdays for House Meetings (including House Prayers); it suited announcements of teams and matches. This divided the week into periods of three days and one day. The first three days could be used to develop a theme; the last day of the week to round it off.

It was, however, a building extension which made delegation necessary. It provided a hall suitable for a separate Sixth Form assembly. At first there was doubt about the wisdom of splitting a school of 900 boys: we tried separate assemblies on Mondays, Tuesdays, and Wednesdays, and a united assembly on Fridays. But the Great Hall, which would hold the 650 Main School boys in seated comfort, was tight when the 250 Sixth Formers returned – the discomfort was more obvious because it was unnecessary. We therefore decided to meet as a whole school only at the beginning and end of each term.

'We shape our buildings, then our buildings shape us', Churchill once said. This is true of school buildings, and also of the pattern of organization adopted. It is important to break cramping patterns and so make possible the maximum development the building allows. Changes take time and imagination; a 'divine discontent' with things as they are is a prime requisite. Full use should then be made of all resources, whether material or human.

Obviously two assemblies running simultaneously require at least two leaders of assembly – it was assumed that the headmaster would always be in either one assembly or the other (though not always as leader). Sometimes a master, or three masters, or maybe a boy or a group of boys, would work out a theme for the first three days of the week, and the headmaster would round it off on the Friday, perhaps hoping to restore a norm if expositions had been lopsided. His job was to be *catholic*, to ensure a balance, to be aware of the total impact of a term's assemblies, to see them as a major educational influence within the school.

One development promised well, though incompatible with the Head's appearance on Fridays at Sixth Form assembly. The Head of Main School planned his assemblies in weekly instalments, telling the headmaster what was happening, and making room for his completing the week's programme on Fridays. There was gradually accumulating a valuable pile of material based on this pattern, Friday's contribution usually bringing out the general principles underlying the incidents and stories heard earlier in the week.

The assumption behind all this is that the headmaster and his senior colleagues care about assembly, see its function in the same way, and have sufficient confidence in each other to be frank about material, resources, and difficulties.

The two assemblies which follow illustrate some of these points.

Each of them followed three which are implied but which are not included here.

Assembly 20, about Sikhism, tells of a particular experience, though the passages quoted can be used by others. Earlier in the year the Senior History master had drafted and produced a threesome on Great Religious Truths:

> Confucius & Reciprocity
> Buddha & Compassion
> Mohammed & Submission

ending with a suggestion that we see their wisdom in the light of *Heb*. 1. 1–3a. Obviously local conditions must be taken into account with a theme of this sort.

Assembly 21 is a Main School assembly, completing a series on Freedom presented earlier in the week. Its contents were decided after consultation with the Head of Main School about what had already been said. Main School assembly includes the singing of a hymn; there is no congregational singing in the Sixth Form assembly.

Assembly 20 (the fourth of a series)
Sikhism

Leader

During the (Easter) vacation I was a guest at the Sikh New Year Celebrations, invited by the Sikh Social and Cultural Society of Huddersfield. The word *Sikh* means disciple, follower – followers of the ten *Gurus* (that is, teachers).

Sikhism was founded by Guru Nanak, born in 1469; he was followed by nine other Gurus; the tenth and last Guru, Guru Gobind Singh, was born in 1666.

Sikhism was founded as a monotheistic reform to embrace Hindu and Muslim in one brotherhood; it deprecates image worship, priestcraft and caste, and lays great stress on ethical virtues.

Though Sikhs neither smoke nor drink alcohol, they made provision for both for their guests at their Celebrations which lasted five hours. Explanations of their teaching and history were given, and hymns were sung to the accompaniment of Sikh music.

We shall hear English translations of the words of two of the hymns which were sung, the first about the universal brotherhood of man, a hymn written by Nanak. The words *Shiahs* and *Sunis* which occur refer to sects of the Muslim religion.

First Reading

One man by shaving his head
Reckons to turn into a holy monk,
Another man sets up as a *Yogi*
Or some other type of ascetic.
Some call themselves *Hindus:*
Others call themselves *Musulmans.*
Among these there are the *Shiahs,*
There are the *Sunis* also,
And yet MAN is of ONE RACE throughout the WORLD;
God as CREATOR and God as GOOD,
God in His BOUNTY and God in His MERCY,
IS ALL ONE GOD.

77

Even in our misconjecture WE MUST NOT discriminate God from God!
Worship the ONE GOD,
For ALL MANKIND the ONE DIVINE TEACHER,
ALL MEN HAVE THE SAME FORM,
ALL RACES OF MAN have the SAME SOUL.

Leader

During the Celebrations, stories were told of the Gurus – traditional tales. When the first Guru, Guru Nanak, who travelled far, wanted to show the falsehood of some Muslim beliefs he *acted* his teaching.

He was near Mecca and knew no Muslim would sleep with his feet pointing to Mecca, the place of God, for that would be a profanation. He, a stranger, feigned sleep, putting himself in the forbidden position, feet to Mecca. He was disturbed by the good Muslims who protested. He asked why, and then said to them: 'Turn me so that my feet point in a direction where God is not', using their consequent perplexity to teach the universality of God's presence.

We shall hear the words of the final hymn sung at the Celebrations.

Second Reading

> Lord, Thou art like a mighty River, All-knowing, All-seeing,
> And I like a tiny fish in Thy vast waters,
> How shall I gauge Thy depths?
> How shall I reach Thy shores?
> Wherever I go, I see Thee only,
> And when snatched out of Thy Waters I die of separation.
> I know not the fisher,
> I see not the net
> But flapping in my agony I call upon Thee for help.
>
> O Lord Who pervadeth ALL things,
> In my fallibility I thought Thou wert far away,
> But no deed I do can ever be out of Thy sight;
> Thou Who art All-Seeing, all things Thou seest:
> I am not worthy to serve Thee,
> Nor do I glory in Thy Name.
>
> Thy gifts are my portion,
> There is no other door
> To which I may go;

This then is the humble prayer
of Thy servant, Nanak:
Accept my mind and my body
As devoted unto Thee.

The Lord is near, the Lord is afar,
The Lord is in the mean between these two extremities;
He watcheth His Creation,
He hears His Creation, for He is the Creator;
Nanak, whatever the Lord wills,
That cometh to pass.

Let us pray

The prayer we shall say is one used by *Toc H*.

O God, who hast made of one blood all nations of men for to dwell on the face of the earth, and who didst send thy blessed Son to preach peace to them that are afar off, and to them that are nigh, grant that all the peoples of the world may seek after thee and find thee; and hasten, O Lord, the fulfilment of thy promise to pour out thy Spirit upon all flesh through Jesus Christ our Lord.   Amen.

The Lord bless us and keep us. The Lord make his face to shine upon us and be gracious unto us. The Lord lift up the light of his countenance upon us, and give us peace. Amen.

Num. 6. 24–26

Assembly 21 (the fourth of a series for the Main School)

Freedom

Leader

The hymn we shall sing was written during the struggle in America for the freeing of the slaves. The tune has some resemblance to *The Minstrel Boy*.

Hymn *Songs of Praise* 306 Men, whose boast it is that ye
                Tune: *Ives*

Leader

During the week you have been thinking about freedom: freedom from prejudice, freedom from hunger, and freedom from fear. All of them, freedom *from* something; about what people want to get away from. And perhaps you, too, think of freedom as getting away from constraints.

The slave feels like that; so does the man in prison. So do you when, quite properly, you are ready to leave school; you look forward to your freedom. You may even feel you want freedom from your homes because you want to stand on your own feet.

But there is another kind of freedom that I want us to consider today. When a man has shed his chains, when he has got out of prison, what does he do next? He has only thought of getting out; now he has to decide for himself. He has to be responsible for his own life, and he has not been used to this.

This second kind of freedom is not *from* anything; it is *for* something: it looks ahead.

Reading

The kingdom of heaven is like treasure hidden in a field, which a man found and covered up; then in his joy he goes and sells all that he has and buys that field.

Again, the kingdom of heaven is like a merchant in search of fine pearls, who, on finding one pearl of great value, went and sold all that he had and bought it.

Matt. 13. 44–46 *RSV*

Leader

The two parables are about the second kind of freedom. It is: having an interest and being able to follow it, having an ability and being able to develop it, seeing a job and wanting to do it, knowing what is worthwhile and being allowed to tackle it. This kind of freedom is positive; it looks ahead – not backwards at constraints – but ahead, ready to grasp opportunities – ready to dig the field, or buy the pearl.

There are, then, freedom *from*, the first kind, and freedom *for*, the second kind. But sometimes all this gets muddled up. The man in prison seems to be freer than the man outside. Paul, in prison, could say 'Rejoice in the Lord alway: and again I say, Rejoice' (*Phil.* 4. 4). Bunyan, in prison, could write *Pilgrim's Progress*. And the man outside seems to be at odds with himself. There is nothing he wants to be free for. And sometimes *we* are at sixes and sevens with ourselves; we are not free. What is wrong is inside us.

You get a picture of this when you get an unexpected afternoon free. Some people at once go to their hobby – stamp-collecting, say. Others don't know what to do with themselves; they hang about just waiting for something to turn up – perhaps they get into trouble just for something to do! They are free, yet not free, because they have found nothing to be free for.

The second kind of freedom is inside you. No wonder one of our prayers speaks of 'whose service is perfect freedom'. And Jesus said: 'You will know the truth, and the truth will make you free' (*John* 8. 32).

Let us pray

Almighty God, in whom we live and move and have our being, who hast made us for thyself so that we can find rest only in thee, grant us purity of heart and strength of purpose, so that no selfish passion shall hinder us from knowing thy will, no weakness keep us from doing it. In thy light may we see light and in thy service find our freedom and our strength, through Jesus Christ our Lord.

Prayers in Use at Uppingham School (modified)

The Lord's Prayer

All   The grace of our Lord Jesus Christ,
and the love of God,
and the fellowship of the Holy Spirit,
be with us all evermore.   Amen.

B · Group Participation

The varied activities of a Sixth Form result in many different groupings of students. Some are associated with specialist studies, some with options in General Studies, some with extra-curricular activities; others relate to administrative tasks, to leadership functions, and to the community service which the school undertakes; yet others are occasional and *ad hoc*, serving particular purposes. Superimposed on this already overlapping pattern are the ordinary friendships which bring students together however different their major concerns may be.

Most of these groupings can make particular contributions to the life of the school, for instance, in the fortnightly exhibitions on the display boards in the entrance hall. Most can be harnessed to enrich assembly. We set out in full a series worked out by an Upper Sixth French set and the Head of the French Department who taught them. Other Departments can contribute along the lines of their specialisms, the exercise of selecting material and of communicating it to others being valuable disciplines. Many of the School's societies can play a part; certainly drama (see Assembly 37, p. 137) and music. Descriptions of welfare services, and of the needs which the school's neighbourhood service units seek to meet, can be an education to those not involved. The school's local history society may be called on – say, to explore local churches and so provide the kind of material used in Assemblies 38–40 (especially p. 147).

Generally speaking, contributions of this sort will not come spontaneously. But once ideas are suggested (maybe to masters at a Staff Meeting), and several groups have performed, others will seek to emulate them.

The series *Four French Authors* provides a case in point; in fact, it followed a series on *Four Russian Authors*. There was considerable initial zeal, much 'research', and afterwards a feeling of achievement when they had done their whack! Records were kept (hence the assemblies given here), but the first rapture will not easily be recaptured. Teachers get used to repeating lessons: each audience is a new one; repetition is never exact, for teaching is a two-way operation. This is harder for boys; the first freshness is quickly spent. But assemblies are not repeated unless, in a modified form, for the Main School. Three years, however, brings a complete change in the Sixth Form population. An idea may be suggested again. But the new students have to do *their* thinking; they cannot copy what has been done before; better that they know nothing about it.

I am happy to acknowledge my indebtedness to Mr J. Gowans and his students of 1966 for the assemblies which follow: translations were a corporate effort.

Assembly 22 (1 of 4)

Four French Authors · 1 Pascal

Leader

The readings this week are by members of Upper Sixth Arts and the music has been chosen by them. The authors are all French but, no doubt, some of you will be relieved to learn that they have been translated, more or less, into English. The choice has not been easy because the field is so wide; but what I suppose distinguishes French literature is that it tends to be intellectual in its approach, and we have concentrated on this aspect.

The remainder of the week will be devoted to twentieth-century writers, but for this morning we have chosen a reading from the seventeenth-century – from the *Pensées* of Blaise Pascal. What is old is not necessarily out-of-date. Pascal's contribution to scientific knowledge was small when we think of the field of science today. He did some experimenting on atmospheric pressure, I believe – went up a mountain with a vacuum, or, rather, sent his brother-in-law up with it, which shows that he had his wits about him. But, of course, we know that he was a man with an enquiring mind who did make an original contribution to scientific knowledge. But it is as a religious thinker and a stylist that he has his place in literature.

He did not have to worry about the hydrogen bomb or the colour problem or conflicting ideologies. He did not even disagree with his Head of State, though he might have done if he had lived much longer; but he had the problems of his time. He was born in 1623 and died in 1662 at the age of 39, and the world then, to a thinking man, must have looked pretty black.

France was rapidly becoming the leading power in Europe, but beneath the dawning splendour of the French monarchy, which was in a few years to reach its zenith in the panoply and glitter of Versailles, there lay much misery and doubt. At a time when civil war raged in England, France too was torn by civil strife in a quarrel which was not illumined by the high principles which ennobled the English struggle. Pascal must have seen on all sides injustice, oppression, corruption, sudden death, and starvation, even mass starvation in one grim winter when wolves entered the suburbs of Paris itself in search of food. If you get the chance to see a French film first shown in this country about ten years ago, called *Monsieur Vincent*, I recommend you to do so. It gives a grim but compelling picture of the times. Life was, for the ordinary man, in the words of Hobbes, 'nasty, brutish, short'.

Pascal wrote two religious works. One, the *Provinciales*, is a witty, amusing, and biting attack on the Jesuits, who might be regarded as the Establishment in the church of the day. Parts of it read rather like the satirical dialogues of the BBC, except that it is much better written. This book, by the way, was burned by the common hangman shortly after Pascal's death, so that if he had lived much longer, he might well have been another scientist imprisoned for deviationist writings.

His second book was a collection of thoughts, *Les Pensées*, which, taken together, attempt to formulate an intellectual basis for Christian belief. I don't think it altogether succeeds. It is too argumentative, and Pascal is a man of his time with the knowledge and prejudices of his age. The historians among you might think, for example, that he shows some bias in his reference to the death of a contemporary Englishman.

'Cromwell', he says, 'would have ravaged the whole of the Christian world, the English royal family would have been destroyed and his own put permanently in power, if a little grain of sand hadn't lodged in his bladder. Rome itself would have trembled beneath his power. But as this little piece of gravel had been put there,' he continues with relish, 'Cromwell is dead, his family disgraced, everything peaceful, and the king back on his throne again.' Quite a few Englishmen would have agreed with him.

Pascal, a contemporary of Descartes and Milton, was a noble and tortured soul. He was comfortably off but his health was poor, and he was deeply engaged in the doctrinal quarrels of his day. Life is never a picnic for the Pascals of this world. Yet, in an age when the underlying mood of literature was pessimism, he envisaged the human condition as something noble. Let us listen to one short *Pensée* of Blaise Pascal.

Reading

Man is but a reed, the feeblest thing in all nature; but he is a thinking reed. It doesn't need the whole universe to rise up and crush him: a puff of wind, a drop of water, is enough to kill him. But even if the universe should crush him, man would still be nobler than that which kills him, because he knows that he dies, and the universe is quite unaware of its vast physical advantage.

All our dignity consists then in thought. That is where our claim to greatness lies, and not in space or time which are beyond us. Let us then work to think well: that is the first moral principle.

From Pascal's Les Pensées

Let us pray

Help us, O Lord, to use aright the powers of mind that thou hast given us. May we know the joy of thinking and learning. Make us wiser by knowing the best thoughts of those who have lived before us. So may we come to understand ourselves and serve our day and generation according to thy will.   Amen.

Music   Berlioz, from *Symphonie Fantastique*

Four French Authors · 2 Roger Martin du Gard

Leader

'To think well: that is the first moral principle', said Pascal. This thought is developed in a twentieth-century context by Roger Martin du Gard in his novel *Les Thibault*, published in 1944, at a time when Europe could see the approach of the final crisis and the end of a catastrophic war. The humiliation of occupation had a profound effect on French thought. The reading which follows and the two remaining readings for this week are all from works published or conceived during the war. When the end came, people all over Europe looked forward to the aftermath with mingled hope and trepidation. So much had been destroyed; what would take its place?

The French have always prided themselves, and rightly so, on their intellectual independence. This has sometimes been obscured by nationalistic fervour, by self-interest, by complacency; but always there have been protesting voices. Listen now to the letter of advice written to the younger Thibault – you can judge for yourselves, twenty years afterwards, how far he was justified in his hopes and fears.

Reading

What I wanted to write to you is this: it seems to me that in the times that are coming, public opinion, and the master ideas that direct it, will have a growing and determining influence. The future will probably be more malleable than it has ever been. The individual will be more important. The man of worth will have, more than in the past, the chance of making himself heard and promoting his ideas, and the possibility of taking part himself in reconstruction.

Grow into a man of worth. Develop in yourself an independent personality. Distrust current theories. It is tempting to shed the exacting burden of being a person in your own right. It is tempting to let yourself be swallowed up in a vast movement of collective enthusiasm. It is tempting to *believe*, because it is easy, and because it is supremely comfortable! Will *you* be able to resist the temptation?

... It won't be easy. The more confused the trails seem to be, the more man is inclined, in order to find a way through at any price, to accept some ready-made doctrine which will reassure and guide him. Any more-or-less plausible reply to the questions he asks himself and which he never manages to solve on his own, is offered to him like an escape, above all if that reply has the weight of majority opinion behind it.

That is the greatest danger. Resist! Reject the popular slogans! Don't let yourself be caught up! It is better to suffer the agonies of uncertainty than to enjoy the sense of lazy moral well-being offered to every follower by the doctrinaires. Feeling your own way through the darkness will be no laughing matter, but it is the least dangerous course. The worst thing you can do is to follow docilely the flags waved by your neighbours.

Let us pray

Deliver us, O God, from following false fashions in our thinking. Save us from the worship of power, whether power over nature or power over men. Save us from the exploiting kind of science which neglects all that is human. Grant that we and all men may learn to use every advance of knowledge for the betterment of mankind. So may we not misuse thy gifts, nor rest in false hopes or misplaced trust, but learn the way which accords with thy will and our salvation, through Jesus Christ our Lord.

Music   from Ravel's *Daphnis et Chloé*
or Debussy's *Prélude à l'après-midi d'un faune*

Four French Authors · 3 Albert Camus

Leader

One of the manifestations of modern French thought is existentialism. There are various brands, Christian and non-Christian. But don't be alarmed! I am not going to attempt to explain them. To be quite honest, I don't think I could. Neither am I going to read to you from any of the hard books on existentialist philosophy; I can't understand them myself.

The best thing to do might be to listen to an extract from a novel by Albert Camus for, in France, ideas are often more palatably propagated through the play and the novel. For example, the best-known existentialist in France is the playwright and novelist Sartre.

Albert Camus was essentially a modern man – I say *was* because he was killed in a car crash in 1960. He was not a Christian, but he was a serious thinker. The rash of 'outsider' literature we have had in this country stems largely from his novel *L'Etranger*.

The reading for today is from a novel published in 1947 called *La Peste*. Note the date, just after the war. The banal, dull, provincial town of Oran in French North Africa has been stricken by that scourge of the Middle Ages, bubonic plague. *La Peste* (*The Plague*) may be viewed in various ways. It is a realistic chronicle of an epidemic in a modern city. Or again, it is the German occupation of Europe. Or again, it is the evil in the heart of man and in the world. Or again, it is an allegory of the human condition.

The inhabitants of Oran are reluctant to see the truth that stares them in the face. The authorities try to play it down: it is merely a fever, a virus; the dead rats in the street are a coincidence. But gradually the truth has to be faced. It is the dreaded plague, and the town is closed to the outside world.

Camus analyzes the reactions of his characters to a meaningless calamity. Some try to escape; others just give up; others look upon it as a judgment; others try to ignore it. But the doctor, Rieux, who knows that he is ultimately powerless, revolts against fate. Existentialism is a literature of revolt.

The characters mentioned in the extract we are going to hear are:

Father Paneloux, the popular preacher who expresses, or rather caricatures, the orthodox church position;
Tarrou, the intellectual, who regards himself as a spectator; and
the doctor, Rieux, who largely represents the author's views.

It is the doctor who actively organizes the resistance to the plague. His friend Tarrou has asked if he can help, and there follows the conversation we are going to hear. Rieux replies to Tarrou:

Reading (two voices and the leader as narrator)

Rieux I need hardly tell you that I accept your suggestion most gladly. One can't have too many helpers. But I take it you know work of this kind may prove fatal to the worker. Have you weighed the dangers?

Tarrou What did you think of Paneloux's sermon, doctor?

Rieux I've seen too much of hospitals to relish any idea of collective punishment. But, as you know, Christians sometimes say that sort of thing without really meaning it.

Tarrou However, you think, like Paneloux, that the plague has its good side; it opens men's eyes and forces them to take thought?

Rieux So does every ill that flesh is heir to. What's true of all the evils in the world is true of plague as well. It helps men to rise above themselves. All the same, when you see the misery it brings, you'd need to be a madman, or a coward, or stone blind, to give in tamely to the plague. . . . But you haven't answered my question yet. Have you weighed the consequences?

Tarrou Do you believe in God, doctor?

Rieux No. But what does that really mean? I'm fumbling in the dark, struggling to make something out. But I've long ceased finding that original . . .

Tarrou Isn't that it? – the gulf between Paneloux and you?

Rieux I doubt it. Paneloux is a man of learning, a scholar. He hasn't come into contact with death; that's why he can speak with such assurance of the truth – with a capital T. But every country priest who visits his parishioners, and has heard a man gasping for breath on his deathbed, thinks as I do. He'd try to relieve human suffering before trying to point out its excellence. Let's drop the subject.

Tarrou My question is this: Why do you yourself show such devotion considering you don't believe in God? I suspect your answer will help me to mine.

Narrator Rieux said that he'd already given the answer; that if he believed in an all-powerful God he would cease curing the sick. But no one in the world believed in such a God. And this was proved by the fact that no one ever threw himself on Providence completely. Anyway, in this respect Rieux believed himself to be on the right road – in fighting against creation as he found it. There speaks the existentialist. He goes on:

Rieux Yes, you're thinking it a mark of pride to feel that way. But, I assure you, I've no more pride than is needed to keep me going. I have no idea what's awaiting me, or what will happen when all this ends. For the moment I know this: there are sick people, and they need curing. Later on, perhaps, they'll think things over; and so shall I. I protect them as best I can; that's all.

Tarrou Against whom?

Rieux I haven't a notion, Tarrou; I assure you, I haven't a notion. When I entered this profession I did it abstractedly so to speak, because I had a desire for it, because it meant a career like another – one that young men often aspire to. Perhaps, too, because it was particularly difficult for a workman's son like myself ... and then I had to see people die. I saw that I could never get hardened to it. I was young then, and I was outraged by the whole scheme of things, or so I thought. Subsequently I grew more modest. Only, I've never managed to get used to seeing people die. That's all I know. Yet after all ...

Tarrou After all?

Rieux After all, since the order of the world is shaped by death, mightn't it be better for God if we refuse to believe in him, and struggle with all our might against death without raising our eyes towards the heaven where he sits in silence?

Tarrou Yes. But your victories will never be lasting.

Rieux Yes, I know that. But it's no reason for giving up the struggle.

Tarrou No reason, I agree.... Only, I can now picture what this plague must mean for you.

Rieux Yes. A never-ending defeat.

From Albert Camus, *La Peste*

Leader

You may think that the bleak philosophy revealed in this dialogue is relieved by the integrity of the doctor, and by the energy with which he serves his fellowmen. The existentialist is often, surprisingly perhaps, a man of action.

Let us pray

For all men of good will, of whatsoever race or creed, we give thanks, O Lord.

Music Debussy, *La Mer* (*Dialogue du vent et de la mer*)

Four French Authors · 4 Gabriel Marcel and Simone Weil

Leader

A hundred years ago, Charles Baudelaire, the first poet of the life of a great city and perhaps the first modern poet, saw this world as a dark reflection of an ideal world. The task of art, he said, especially of poetry and music, is to break through the dividing barriers between the two worlds.

I would have liked to have read some poetry, for poetry can evoke sensations which are beyond the powers of prose, but it is difficult, if not impossible, to convey the magic of poetry in translation. So, for this morning, in place of the author we had chosen, we shall hear prose readings, two of them, which show an awareness of values which transcend time and place. The first is by the Christian existentialist, Gabriel Marcel.

First Reading

The greatest joy I knew when I was a child was in discovering, exploring, imagining beyond what I could see, in planning other more distant, fuller voyages! And, later on, what a delight it was to me to read those pages in which Proust describes how words crystallize around imagined sensations! All that meant more to me than I can say, and revealed a marked fondness for the unfamiliar, the inaccessible, and a contempt which shocks me today for what is within everyone's reach, for what everyone has seen – such as Versailles, or Mont St Michel.

The words vanity, snobbery, come naturally to me when I recall my childhood's state of mind. However, when I really think about it, I believe I can see the origins of this propensity in something else: in the horror of seeing innocence soiled, in the ingenuous and absurd idea that what is distant in space is also something which has not been trampled underfoot, has not been profaned, something with which the mind can form an intimate and intoxicating alliance, whereas the near, the familiar, is adulterated and soiled by the layer of stereotyped adjectives which each visitor has heaped upon it – for is not Hohenschwangau, after all, to the Munich shopkeeper, just what Versailles is to the Parisian?

But, despite all this, I don't think I am wrong in seeing in this attitude the metaphysical urge to discover something familiar and meaningful at the heart of the most distant things, the urge, that is to say, not to triumph externally over space by speed, but to tear out its spiritual and secret meaning which would reduce to nothingness its physical remoteness. I don't think I was ever very impressed by speed; what counted for me was to discover a 'somewhere else' that could become, in essence, a 'here'.

From *Existentialisme Chrétien*

Leader

The second reading is from the writings of a woman, Simone Weil, and was written in 1942. She was a brilliant student and later became a history teacher at a French Lycée where she wrote a number of historical and philosophical essays. She spent a year in Spain during the Civil War and then a year as a factory hand to gain first-hand experience of industrial conditions. The result was her book called *The Industrial Worker* which is, at the moment, on the new book shelves of the French section of the Public Library. The extract we are going to hear is from the beginning of an essay called *A Draft for a Statement of Human Obligations*.

Second Reading

There is a reality outside the world, that is to say, outside space and time, beyond man's mental horizons, beyond any sphere that human faculties can reach out to.

Corresponding to this reality, at the very centre of the human heart, is the longing for an absolute good, a longing which is always there and is never satisfied by any object in this world.

Another terrestrial manifestation of this reality lies in the absurd and insoluble contradictions which are the inevitable result of human thought when it moves exclusively in this world.

Just as the reality of this world is the sole basis of fact, so that other reality is the sole basis of good.

Let us pray

O God, the living God, who hast put thine own eternity in our hearts, and hast made us to hunger and thirst after thee: Satisfy,

we pray thee, the instincts which thou hast implanted in us, that we may find thee in life, and life in thee; through Jesus Christ our Lord.
From Milner-White & Briggs, *Daily Prayer*, OUP, 1941

(The French Assistant then says the Lord's Prayer)

Notre Père, qui es aux cieux, Que ton Nom soit sanctifié. Que ton règne vienne. Que ta volonté soit faite sur la terre, Comme au ciel. Donne-nous aujourd'hui notre pain quotidien. Et pardonne-nous nos offenses, Comme nous pardonnons à ceux qui nous ont offensés. Et ne nous induis point en tentation; Mais délivre-nous du mal: Car c'est à toi qu'appartiennent le règne, Et la puissance et la gloire, Aux siècles des siècles. Amen.

Que la grâce de notre Seigneur Jésus-Christ, l'amour de Dieu, et la communication du Saint-Esprit soient avec nous tous eternellement. Amen.

Music Berlioz: *Adieu des bergers* from *L'Enfance du Christ*

C · Audience Participation

Is it possible to involve everybody in an active way in assembly? Or are most students to be hearers of the word only, even though the vocalists sing and the readers declaim? In churches, public worship includes some congregational activity – hymns, responses, above all the drama of the breaking of bread. Are there any equivalents when Sixth Formers don't sing hymns and are reluctant to join in responsive prayers?

There can be no doubt that active participation is desirable, but the difficulties are obvious. Eight to twelve is the optimum size for a discussion group; thirty is the size for secondary school teaching, and perhaps the largest for an effective committee. A Sixth Form assembly is likely to include several hundred, fitted together compactly, formally, in rows. These are scarcely the conditions for a good conference; certainly not for individual contributions in assembly.

I have not myself used Assemblies 26–28; I include them because they might suggest further experimenting. I owe their plan to the Rev. J Kenneth Lawton (formerly secretary of the Social Responsibility Department of the British Council of Churches), and it was only after I had retired from headmastering that I attended services in which he used it. An element of improvisation is called for (to weave the unexpected into the pattern), and confidence in the leader of assembly (in both senses); also goodwill (for there is room for ribaldry!). But when the corporate act is an accepted thing the method is worth a trial; it is not for every day.

The particular passages which I have chosen to illustrate this discussion method are not heavily theological, nor do they require much knowledge of ancient history or practice. If utterances of the prophets were handled in this fashion, it would be necessary to recognize that a short assembly is neither the right time for linguistic study, nor for theological depth, nor for social anthropology, nor even for seeing selected passages fully in context. Rather, the intention would be to use the words as a starting point for constructive thought about present circumstances, about ourselves.

These assemblies require a good deal of prior thought both in regard to content and to tidy managing. Not all of the elements (*a*), (*b*), (*c*) need be included. Element (*c*) requires that the leader takes the two or three boys into his confidence on the previous day, telling them the passage to be considered. They should not confer with each other, nor with the leader, before the assembly; a degree of spontaneity is essential. But conciseness should be insisted on lest proceedings be unduly prolonged. The leader should have his own store of ideas from which to draw in order to bind together into a unity the several strands which students contribute. The technique is common enough in the classroom.

Assembly 26 (1 of 3)

Audience Participation: Proverbs · 1 The tongue

As students enter either *they should be given a copy of the proverb* or *they should see it written on a blackboard.*

> A gentle answer is a quarrel averted;
> a word that gives pain does but fan
> the flame of resentment (*Prov.* 15. 1 *Knox*).

1. INTRODUCTION

Leader

The New Testament book most like the Old Testament is probably the letter of James. James says of the tongue: Mankind can tame every kind of beast, but no human being has ever found out how to tame the tongue. The passage begins like this:

Reading

We are betrayed, all of us, into many faults; and a man who is not betrayed into faults of the tongue must be a man perfect at every point, who knows how to curb his whole body. Just so we can make horses obey us, and turn their whole bodies this way and that, by putting a curb in their mouths. Or look at ships; how huge they are, how boisterous are the winds that drive them along! And yet a tiny rudder will turn them this way and that, as the captain's purpose will have it. Just so, the tongue is a tiny part of our body, and yet what power it can boast! How small a spark it takes to set fire to a vast forest! And that is what the tongue is, a fire.

James 3. 2–6a *Knox*

2. PARTICIPATION

(a) Reflection

Leader

I want us to consider the verse in front of us taken from the book of Proverbs. I want each one of you to think of the most significant instance or application of it in your own life or in the life of the school, and then of what the verse means in added wisdom. We shall spend two minutes in silence while individually we reflect on its meaning.

(*b*) *Sharing*

Leader

And now will each of you quietly share with your neighbour your thoughts on the passage. Pair off in the most convenient way.

(*c*) *Public commentary*

Leader

Before I ask three (or two) prefects to share with us their thinking I would like to read two further verses from *James* about the tongue:

> We use it to bless God who is our Father; we use it to curse our fellow men, that were made in God's image; blessing and cursing come from the same mouth.
>
> *James* 3. 9, 10a *Knox*

And now the three prefects: (Each, in turn, expresses concisely one or two thoughts on the passage).

3. SUMMING UP

Leader (Necessarily improvising, and basing his comment on what the prefects have said. The following ideas may have occurred, or some of them may be introduced.)

Some of you see the passage as being about school discipline – a good prefect or master gets what he wants without using words that provoke resentment.

Or it means 'peace at any price', or just 'oiling the wheels of life'.

Or it is about a personal experience, some words said, which you regret, from which you have learned something about other people's psychology and your own.

You may remember the Hebrew law: 'Thou shalt not go up and down as a talebearer among thy people' (*Lev.* 19. 16), or the passage containing the sentence, 'Out of the abundance of the heart the mouth speaketh' (*Matt.* 12. 33–37), or that it was said of Jesus, 'They wondered at the gracious words which proceeded out of his mouth' (*Luke* 4. 22).

Or again, the greater danger of putting the unkind remark into writing, for that makes it permanent and it can be pored over so creating endless bitterness.

The comments might well end by quoting the verse which follows the passage:

> The speech of the wise is learning's ornament;
> the fool babbles on (*Prov.* 15. 2).

Let us pray

Let the words of my mouth, and the meditation of my heart, be acceptable in thy sight, O Lord, my strength, and my redeemer.

Ps. 19. 14

> God be in my head, and in my understanding;
> God be in my eyes, and in my looking;
> God be in my mouth, and in my speaking;
> God be in my heart, and in my thinking;
> God be at mine end, and at my departing.
> *Horae B. V. Mariae* (London, 1514)

Let the words of my mouth, and the meditation of my heart, be acceptable in thy sight, O Lord, my strength, and my redeemer.

Assembly 27 (2 of 3)

Audience Participation: Proverbs · 2 Careers

As students enter either *they should be given a copy of the proverb* or *they should see it written on a blackboard.*

> Better dry crust and gay heart,
> than a house where all is feasting
> and all is quarrelling (*Prov.* 17. 1 *Knox*).

1. INTRODUCTION

Leader

Today we shall think about careers, the ends to which our ambitions are directed, and what it is that we most value when we think of our own futures. We shall use the verse from *Proverbs* as our starting point.

It is easy to accept conventional standards of success; not so easy to see what they leave out. There is a good deal of emptiness in many lives, even their struggles are at a superficial level. Most of the time we ourselves are content to look one step ahead; let us, today, look a little further.

But first we shall hear a piece of gentle satire, already familiar to some of you, and to well-nigh every university student.

Recording

Little Boxes, as sung by Pete Seeger (about 1¾ minutes). Band 2 on Side 1 of the 7-inch CBS record AGG 320055 (Pete Seeger in Concert).

2. PARTICIPATION

(a) Reflection

Leader

As yesterday, we shall spend two minutes thinking about the verse, about dry crusts and feasting, noting how its wisdom accords with, or conflicts with, our own half-formulated ideas. Try to crystallize out in words your own reactions to the verse.

(*b*) *Sharing*

Leader

And now will each of you quietly share with your neighbour the ideas you have formulated. Pair off in the most convenient way.

(*c*) *Public commentary*

Leader

I asked two (or three) of you to think about this verse, giving you longer notice. I do not know what particular reactions you will express, but let me first remind you of a parable of Jesus which is consistent with the ancient wisdom of our verse from *Proverbs*.

Jesus spake a parable, saying, The ground of a certain rich man brought forth plentifully:

And he thought within himself, saying, What shall I do, because I have no room where to bestow my fruits?

And he said, This will I do: I will pull down my barns, and build greater; and there will I bestow all my fruits and my goods.

And I will say to my soul, Soul, thou hast much goods laid up for many years; take thine ease, eat, drink, and be merry.

But God said unto him, Thou fool, this night thy soul shall be required of thee: then whose shall those things be, which thou hast provided?

So is he that layeth up treasure for himself, and is not rich toward God.

Luke 12. 16–21 *AV*

And now for the two (or three) of you ready to share your thinking with the rest of us, whether or not it fits in with the parable:

(Each, in turn, expresses concisely one or two thoughts on the proverb.)

3. SUMMING UP

Leader (Necessarily improvising, and basing his comments on what the students have said. The following ideas may have occurred, or some of them may be introduced.)

Some of you will think that what matters in a career is the money you will get – where will you get most? Money *is* important; but there are other things, the proverb says.

But you cannot have a gay heart if you only have a crust! Basic needs must come first, and these are increasing all the time. Anyway, the gay heart is just a matter of temperament.

What matters is prospects, not initial salary: prospects in the sense of whether the job will give you the personal satisfactions you expect, measuring up to your abilities, interests and ideals for yourself. (And here could come in all the advice of a careers master!) 'Personal fulfilment is the function of an adequate personal ideal freely chosen, not the fantasy of living out every possibility' (Charles Davis).

The important thing is personal relations; the home you make matters more than your job.

'You cannot serve God and mammon' (*Matt.* 6. 24).

Is 'Do as little as you can for as much as you can get' a formula for happiness; if not, why not?

When you are young, what matters is present enjoyment; you cannot look ahead, for every step forward alters your horizons.

Why not look at those older people you most admire who seem to be happy? What spirit informs their living?

Let us pray

Almighty God, who art the source of all our life, grant us the power to advance in all things that are good. And in all our getting may we get wisdom – the vision to discern, and the purpose to follow after, the things that are of truest worth; through Jesus Christ our Lord.

H. Bisseker (shortened)

All   The grace of our Lord Jesus Christ,
                and the love of God,
                and the fellowship of the Holy Spirit,
            be with us all evermore. Amen.

Assembly 28 (3 of 3)

Audience Participation: Proverbs · 3 Values

As students enter either *they should be given a copy of the proverb* or *they should see it written on a blackboard.*

> Man's heart is ever full of devising; from the Lord comes the ordering of right speech (*Prov.* 16. 1 *Knox*).

I. INTRODUCTION
Leader
What is our philosophy of life, the standard by which we judge the worth of things? Is it pleasure, or money, or love of power? Is the greatest happiness of the greatest number a sufficient guide to live by? Or are there absolute values which we should acknowledge for our good? – Man's devising, or the Lord's ordering?

Before we consider these questions we shall hear a few stanzas of an American hymn written at the beginning of this century by a man who, though without much in the way of Christian orthodoxy, yet felt that Right is somehow at the heart of the universe.

Solo Voice

> When the anchors that faith had cast
>   Are dragging in the gale,
> I am quietly holding fast
>   To the things that cannot fail.
>
> I know that right is right;
>   That it is not good to lie;
> That love is better than spite,
>   And a neighbour than a spy.
>
> I know that passion needs
>   The leash of a sober mind;
> I know that generous deeds
>   Some sure reward will find.
>
> In the darkest night of the year,
>   When the stars have all gone out,
> That courage is better than fear,
>   That faith is truer than doubt;

> And fierce though the fiends may fight,
>   And long though the angels hide,
> I know that Truth and Right
>   Have the universe on their side.
>
> And that somewhere, beyond the stars,
>   Is a Love that is better than fate;
> When the night unlocks her bars,
>   I shall see Him, and I will wait.
>
> Washington Gladden, 1836–1918

(This can be sung to the chant tune *Mornington*, Ancient Hymns and Canticles, No. 45, in the Methodist Hymn Book.)

2. PARTICIPATION

(a) Reflection

Leader

And now I would ask each of you to think of what you regard as a basis for living. Is all we have 'Man's heart, ever full of devising': hedonism, utilitarianism, enlightened self-interest? Or are there absolutes to be discovered, or, that have been revealed? Try to put into a single sentence what you think.

(b) Sharing

Leader

And now will each of you quietly share with your neighbour the ideas you have formulated. Pair off in the most convenient way.

(c) Public commentary

Two students (as in the previous assemblies) state their viewpoints. (If with opposed viewpoints, so much the better.)

3. SUMMING UP

Leader

(Again improvisation will be necessary, and perhaps some linking with General Studies.) The following points might be useful:

(i) An anecdote: In his *Autobiography*, Charles Darwin tells how an inventor friend (Charles Babbage, 1792–1871) saw a pump at the roadside in Italy. An inscription said the pump was erected for the love of God and his country, and that the tired wayfarer might drink. The inventor was curious and examined the pump closely. He soon discovered that every time that a wayfarer pumped some water for himself, he pumped a larger quantity into the owner's house.

(ii) A reading: *Wisd.* 8. 21–9. 6 (*Knox*).

(iii) Reference might be made to Paul's 'every wind of doctrine' phrase (*Eph.* 4. 14 in the context of verses 1–7, 11–16), or to the two-foundations parable (*Matt.* 7. 24–27), or to the verses which follow the proverb, especially verse 3: Share with the Lord the burden of all thy doings, if thou wouldst be sincere in thy intent.

Let us pray

Save us, O Lord, from being tossed to and fro and carried about with every wind of doctrine. Grant us to see all our decisions in the light of thy will for us, that the house that we build may have its foundations on the rock and not on the sand, through Jesus Christ our Lord.

D · *Behind-the-Scenes Participation*

We had spent several days on Paul's famous passage on charity. On the first day we had heard some of its phrases spoken antiphonally in three translations, thus (I *Cor.* 13. 6):

Voice 1 Love is never glad when others go wrong, love is gladdened by goodness.
Voice 2 (Charity) rejoiceth not in iniquity, but rejoiceth in the truth.
Voice 3 (Love) does not gloat over other men's sins, but delights in the truth.

The versions here are Moffat's, the Authorized Version, and the New English Bible. It was after hearing this that a colleague brought to me the following delightful period piece. (He had no knowledge of the source.) I *Cor.* 13 – an eighteenth-century translation:

Benevolence is unruffled, is benign: Benevolence cherishes no ambitious desires: Benevolence is not ostentatious; is not inflated with insolence.
It preserves a consistent decorum; is not enslaved to sordid interest;

is not transported with furious passion; indulges no malevolent designs.

It conceives no delight from the perpetration of wickedness; but is the first to applaud truth and virtue.

It throws a veil of candour over all things.

For in this state our knowledge is defective, our prophetic powers are limited.

In fine, the virtues of superior eminence are these three, faith, hope, benevolence – but the most illustrious of these is benevolence.

This is an example of behind-the-scenes participation and support. It means that the attitude to assembly is positive; that it is a valued part of the school's life. When it is known that the headmaster is on the look-out for ideas and material, not to ease his tasks (for it does not necessarily do this), but to enrich the school's worship and to involve others, then a school responds.

Another illustration is seen in the way in which singing in the twentieth-century idiom is accepted in assembly. For instance, in the pre-Easter week in one year, we included:

1. Recorded music from *A Man Dies* (Ewan Hooper and Ernest Marvin, Darton, Longman & Todd). We used Items 1, 14, 4 (in this order) on side 2 of Columbia 33SX1609. This was as effective in the Main School as it was with the Sixth Form.
2. Excerpts from Colin Davis's *Messiah* (Items 22, 23 on side 4 of SAL 3584–6) used with readings from Mark's story in the Phillips' translation.
3. Live singing from *Songs from Notting Hill* following a further reading from Mark's story. The Senior Mathematics master sang, to his own guitar accompaniment, *Crucify that Man*. (*Songs from Notting Hill* can be obtained from Notting Hill Methodist Church, Lancaster Road, London, W.11.)

Following this, many suggestions were made. We had already used some of Sydney Carter's *Songs of Faith and Doubt* sung by Donald Swann (on EAF 48, a 7-inch Argo record). Other discs were suggested, and such publications as the collections of folk songs *Faith, Folk & Clarity* and *Faith, Folk & Nativity* (Galliard Ltd., Queen Anne's Road, Great Yarmouth).

But recommendations of other sorts of recorded music came in for use in Assembly. One such was of 'subdued and meditative' music and included:

Mozart: Piano Concerto No. 20, 2nd movement
Mozart: Violin Concerto No. 3, 2nd movement
Mozart: Violin Concerto No. 4, 2nd movement
Bach: Chorale Prelude *Wachet auf*
Beethoven: Violin Concerto in D, 2nd movement
Beethoven: Piano Concerto No. 4, 1st movement
Beethoven: Piano Concerto No. 5, 2nd movement
Beethoven: String Quartet, Op. 127, 2nd movement
Elgar: Enigma Variations – *Nimrod*
Schubert: Piano Sonata in B flat, D. 960, 2nd movement
Dvorak: Serenade for Strings, 1st movement

Ideas usually come from the teaching staff rather than from students, though students may be involved in working out the ideas. They may bring to the common store their own private reading, or their special interests, or even holiday incidents. 'I would like to do three assemblies about outstanding Old Boys', the Senior History master said, and very valuable they proved to be. Useful, also, are church publications which explore new methods of worship, for instance, *Worship for Today: suggestions & ideas*, ed. Richard Jones (Epworth Press, 1968); and, for material, study courses such as *Faith, Work and Worship*, the adult course in the *Partners in Learning* series (various publishers including the Religious Education Press, 1968).

Neighbouring schools can often usefully share experiences, though conditions are likely to vary considerably. As I was drafting this chapter, I heard that a nearby girls' school was doing a series based on Erik Routley's 'Historical Survey of Hymns and their Tunes' in *Hymns for Church and School* (the fourth edition of the Public School Hymn Book, Novello, 1964), illustrating the theme by their own singing. And another school was using the BBC publication *Ten to Eight* with profit. I have myself frequently recorded a suitable ten-to-eight talk at the following morning's ten-to-seven repeat, and subsequently used it in assembly.

When students make recommendations the leader may have to do some vetting of the proposed draft – else the material may be too emotional, or too fundamentalist, or too highbrow, or too exhaustive of its theme. But this is an important educational opportunity, as indeed is the whole of school worship. What is important is to value such suggestions. Assembly is *of* the school, not *for* the school.

V *Bible Themes*

How is the bible to be used in assembly? Not via a lectionary, even though it is a major source-book! Too often it is thought of as 'kids' stuff', something to grow out of, a source-book, only, for improving stories. Yet it provides the major archetypes of every fundamental kind of human experience, and unless students get through to this, they miss its significance for their own growth.

The best illustration is in how the New Testament uses the story of the call of Abraham. The story is not only idealized; it becomes both poetry and psychology when it tells of Abraham who 'looked forward to the city which has foundations, whose builder and maker is God' (*Heb.* 11. 10), archetype of every 'call' of faith. (In assembly, John Masefield's poem *The Seekers* could also be used.)

The language of Christian devotion is full of this kind of usage of the old stories. They gather round themselves the accumulation of generations of emotional force and become more important than the first historical occasion would ever warrant. Think of how hymns use the language of the deliverance of the Hebrews from Egypt, elaborating every detail of the story, going far beyond Paul who speaks of Christ, our paschal lamb, sacrificed for us (I *Cor.* 5. 7). The old stories are more than the 'types' of fundamentalist theology; they stand for basic patterns of human experience. They are as fundamental as the story of Oedipus, and are not only explanatory of past experience, but pointers to new experience.

Many, returning to the bible, first discover this significance in the story of Job. But this is how the whole bible should be understood, when once the student has escaped from ancient history and linguistics. We have already indicated it in the notes on Assemblies 9–12 (p. 47), and it is basic to this chapter.

But school worship is not the place for a systematic study of the

Old Testament in this way; that is for Religious Studies (perhaps the general Religious Studies of everybody rather than the specialist Religious Knowledge of A-level syllabuses as most are constituted at present). Further, the New Testament is more important than the Old Testament: it tells of 'the Word that became flesh and dwelt among us'. And here every teaching device has to be used to give freshness to an oft-told tale. Especially, the leader of assembly must start from where students are, at the place of their presuppositions, prejudices, and concerns.

Assembly 29 (1 of 7)

Introduction to the Gospel · 1 Leo and Echinus

It is assumed that this series is given in January

Leader

In the season between Christmas and Easter comes the life and ministry of Jesus Christ, who stands at the centre of the Christian faith.

During this week we shall read about Jesus – from the twelfth century, from the twentieth century, from the nineteenth century; one theme, but disparate readings.

Our twelfth-century reading is from a *Latin Bestiary*, a book of beasts – translated, of course.

A Bestiary is a serious work of natural history, but it belongs to its period. In the so-called 'age of faith', people believed that the universe was governed by a controlling mind; everything meant something. It would be frivolous to study without finding out this meaning. Indeed, symbolism was so important that it did not matter, St Augustine said, whether certain animals existed; what did matter was what they meant.

From many animals we shall consider two: the lion and the sea-urchin.

(The readings are from T. H. White's *The Book of Beasts*, Jonathan Cape, 1954.)

First Reading

Leo the Lion, mightiest of beasts, will stand up to anybody.

They say that the litters of these creatures come in threes. The short ones with curly manes are peaceful: the tall ones with plain hair are fierce.

The nature of their brows and tail-tufts is an index to their disposition. Their courage is seated in their hearts, while their constancy is in their heads. They fear the creaking of wheels, but are frightened by fires even more so.

Scientists say the Leo has three principal characteristics.

His first feature is that he loves to saunter on the tops of mountains. Then, if he should happen to be pursued by hunting men, the smell of the hunters reaches up to him, and he disguises his spoor behind him with his tail. Thus the sportsmen cannot track him.

It was in this way our Saviour (i.e. the Spiritual Lion of the Tribe of Judah, the Rod of Jesse, the Lord of Lords, the Son of God) once hid the spoor of his love in the high places, until, being sent by the Father, he came down into the womb of the Virgin Mary and saved the human race which had perished. Ignorant of the fact that his spoor could be concealed, the Devil (i.e. the hunter of humankind) dared to pursue him with temptations like a mere man. Even the angels themselves who were on high, not recognizing his spoor, said to those who were going up with him when he ascended to his reward: 'Who is this King of Glory?'

The Lion's second feature is, that when he sleeps, he seems to keep his eyes open.

In this very way, Our Lord also, while sleeping in the body, was buried after being crucified – yet his Godhead was awake. As it is said in the *Song of Songs*, 'I am asleep and my heart is awake', or, in the Psalm, 'Behold, he that keepeth Israel shall neither slumber nor sleep.'

The third feature is this, that when a lioness gives birth to her cubs, she brings them forth dead and lays them up lifeless for three days – until their father, coming on the third day, breathes in their faces and makes them alive.

Just so did the Father Omnipotent raise Our Lord Jesus Christ from the dead on the third day. Quoth Jacob: 'He shall sleep like a lion, and the lion's whelp shall be raised.'

So far as their relations with men are concerned, the nature of lions is that they do not get angry unless they are wounded.

Any decent human ought to pay attention to this. For men do get angry when they are not wounded, and they oppress the innocent although the law of Christ bids them to let even the guilty go free.

The compassion of lions, on the contrary, is clear from innumerable examples – for they spare the prostrate; they allow such captives as they come across to go back to their own country; they prey on men rather than on women, and they do not kill children except when they are very hungry. (from pages 7–9)

Second Reading

Echinus (pron. Ek-ī'-nus) the Sea-Urchin is said to be a poor, paltry, and contemptible animal. He is very frequently the herald of a coming tempest to sailors, or the announcer of a calm. When he senses a storm of wind he seizes a stout stone and carries it as ballast, or drags it as an anchor, so as not to be tossed about by the waves. Thus he is saved, not by his own strength, but held firm by an outside help and by the weight which he carries. Sailors snatch eagerly at this information as a sign of the coming disturbance and take care that no hurricane shall suddenly find them unprepared.

What mathematician, what astrologer, or what Chaldean can understand the course of the stars or the movement and signs of the heavens so well? By what natural quality does the sea-urchin comprehend what is taught among us by learned men? Who was the interpreter to it of so great an augury?

Men often see the disorder of the atmosphere and are deceived – for the clouds frequently disperse without a storm. Echinus is not deceived, the signs never escape Echinus. There is so much science in this one poor animal that it foretells the future. Since there is nothing more in it than this one bit of wisdom, we must believe that it is through the tenderness of God to all things that the urchin also gets his function of prescience. Moreover, if God makes lovely the grass of the field so that we marvel; if he feeds the birds and provides food for the ravens, whose young are truly turned toward the Lord; if he gave women the knowledge of weaving and does not leave even the spider destitute of that wisdom, who now minutely and skilfully hangs his roomy webs in the doorways; if God himself gives courage to the horse and unharnesses fear from his neck – so that he leaps about on the plains and is pleasing to kings as he gallops – that horse that detects war from a distance by the smell, and is excited by the sound of the trumpet; and if there are so many unreasoning things and others of no account, such as herbs, such as the lilies which are filled with the ordering of their own knowledge; can we doubt then that he also assigns to Echinus the service of this foresight? God leaves nothing unexplored, nothing unnoticed. He who feeds all things sees all things. He completes all things in wisdom. As it is written: 'He makes everything with knowledge.'

And thus, if he does not neglect poor, blind Echinus, if he takes care of him and trains him in the signs of the future, will he not carefully consider your things too, O Man? Indeed, he truly takes care of you when his divine wisdom is called upon, saying: 'If he has regard to the birds of the air, if he feeds them, are you not more than they? If God adorns the grass of the field, which today is and tomorrow is cast into the fire, how much more will he consider you, O ye of little faith?'

(from pages 212, 213)

Leader

Our prayer has something of the faith in an underlying providence which marked the Bestiary, but is without its moralizing fancifulness.

Let us pray

O God our Father, in whom we live and move and have our being, open our eyes that we may ever behold thy fatherly presence about us. Draw our hearts to thee with the power of thy love. Teach us to be anxious for nothing and, when we have done what thou hast given us to do, help us to leave the issue to thy wisdom. Take from us doubt and mistrust. Lift our thoughts up to thee in heaven, and make us to know that all things are possible to us through thy Son, our Saviour Jesus Christ.

New Every Morning

Grace to you and peace from God the Father, and our Lord Jesus Christ. *Amen.*

Introduction to the Gospel · 2 The Historical Jesus

Leader

Yesterday we read from *The Book of Beasts*, from a time when faith was easy, and was mixed with much fancifulness.

What of us today? Now it is doubt that is easy. Has faith been eaten away by what was called, a generation ago, the 'acids of modernity'? Can we honestly face all that teases the mind, and yet believe?

> Much will depend on what you mean by belief –
> If you mean: *not* a series of propositions to be accepted,
>   *but* a confident open-ness of spirit to things of God,
> I think the answer is YES.

A recent book which summarizes historical research has been translated from the German: Heinz Zahrnt's *The Historical Jesus*. It asks the right historical questions and surveys the field. In the passage we shall hear, the phrase *Son of God* is considered.

Reading

For as long as Jesus Christ has been proclaimed in the world he has been continually put on trial, in different ways, on different charges, and before changing courts and authorities. Most recently he has been arraigned before the court of history. . . .

The sharp draught of modern historical understanding has torn the golden veil which used to be spread over Jesus and the bible and wafted it away. By doing this, however, it has once again brought home to us the nature of Christianity and has shed light on its characteristic, specifically Christian, elements, in a way which has not happened for a long time, perhaps never before. It has not destroyed the revelation of God; it has once again set this revelation free. It has freed it from the suspicion that it is a mere semblance and has returned to it its full historicity. At last the iconography, the secret docetism, which did not take the humanity of Jesus seriously, is gone for ever.

Jesus Christ is now no longer a phantom, no longer a shadowy fairy-tale figure, half man and half God. He is a real historical man who took upon himself the whole fate of a man in this world. . . .

But was Jesus not the 'Son of God'? And even if he himself did not use this title, was not the community right in conferring it upon him? . . .

It must be said from the start that the phrase 'Jesus is the Son of God', taken by itself, can be as misunderstood as an ideology as any phrase in the writings of, say, Karl Marx. And indeed this phrase is misunderstood frequently enough in our communities.

Secondly, we must remember that like all the images and terms which we use to describe God or anything pertaining to God, the term 'Son of God' is a 'symbol'. Now the symbol is distorted and the reality which it represents is lost, if it is understood literally, if for example the situation of a human family is projected into the inner life of God. For this reason we must firmly repudiate any kind of physical or even physiological conceptions which suppose Jesus' divine Sonship to be a special physical quality. They are quite pagan. Of course it cannot be denied that such pagan conceptions haunt the minds of many pious people who clutch so frantically at the phrase 'Son of God'. . . .

What then?

Certainly Jesus Christ is, as they say, 'more than a man'. But this being 'more than a man' does not lie outside and beyond his humanity but in it, in its ultimate depths . . . the understanding of Jesus as Son of God involves nothing 'suprahistorical', 'supernatural', or even unnatural: it must keep us within the sphere of human history. Jesus is the Son of God not through a special act of procreation, and thus through a special physical quality, but through his special attitude within history. Jesus Christ is the Son because he alone allows God really to be his Father. Or we could put it this way: Jesus is the only one who completely fulfils the first commandment by really fearing, loving and trusting God above all things. Jesus is *the* believer. We meet the same picture over and over again in the New Testament evidence: here are the actions and words of one who is all-receiving, who knows himself at every moment to be utterly dependent upon God without any reservations, who is completely given, open and accessible to him. . . .

As the Fourth Gospel says over and over again, Jesus has 'nothing of himself'. But in having nothing of himself, he has everything of God. And precisely in this he proves to be the 'Son'.

from pages 139–143, Heinz Zahrnt,
The Historical Jesus, Collins, 1963

Let us pray

    Save us, O Lord, from reluctance to grow up,
        from the spiritual malaise which refuses to take issues seriously.
    Grant that we may be honest in all our doubts;
        and honest, too, in our feeling after goodness,
        and in our search for truth;
    lest, by acquiescing in easy scepticism,
        we deny to ourselves the way to understanding.

And now a prayer by Erasmus:

    O Lord Jesus Christ, who art the way, the truth and the life, we pray thee suffer us not to stray from thee who art the way, nor to distrust thee who art the truth, nor to rest in any other thing than thee, who art the life. Teach us by thy Holy Spirit what to believe, what to do, and wherein to take our rest. For thy name's sake we ask it. *Amen.*

Introduction to the Gospel · 3 Tolstoy

Leader

It is possible to be fascinated by the quaintness of the *Bestiary*, or to be engrossed by the problems of historical criticism with all its technical apparatus and, in either case, to miss the meaning of the gospel story.

Today's passage is from the writings of Tolstoy. Leo Tolstoy was born in 1828 and died in 1910. He is best known for his great novel *War and Peace*, and he was, an encyclopedia will tell you: novelist, social reformer, religious teacher.

Our reading tells how, late in life, though prosperous and famous, he sought the meaning of life in the gospels. Especially, he came to value the Sermon on the Mount. Hear how he describes this discovery:

Reading

I lived to the age of fifty thinking that the life a man lives from his birth till his death constitutes his whole existence, and that therefore his aim should be to secure happiness for this mortal life. I tried to secure that happiness, but the longer I lived the more evident it became that such happiness does not and cannot exist. The happiness I sought did not come to me, and what I did attain immediately ceased to be happiness as soon as I had attained it. My unhappiness became greater and greater and the inevitability of death more and more apparent, and I understood that in this meaningless and unhappy life nothing awaited me but sufferings, sickness, old age, and destruction. I asked myself: Why is this so? and received no reply. And I came to despair.

What some men said to me and what I myself sometimes tried to believe, namely, that one should not desire happiness for oneself alone but for others – those near to us and all men – did not satisfy me: first because I could not sincerely desire happiness for other people in the way that I did for myself, and secondly and chiefly because those others were doomed to unhappiness and death just as I was, and so all my efforts for their happiness would be in vain.

I came to despair. But I thought that my despair might be the result of my being an exceptional man, and that other men know why they live, and therefore do not despair.

I began to observe other men, but the others did not know why they were living any more than I did. They tried by the bustle of life to stifle this ignorance; some assured themselves and others that they believed in the different religions that had been instilled into them from childhood – but to believe in what they believed in was impossible, it was too stupid. Yes, and many of them, it seemed to me, only pretended to believe, while in the depth of their souls they did not do so.

I could no longer continue to absorb myself in the bustle of life: no bustle could hide the question that continually presented itself to me, and I was unable to begin to believe afresh in the faith taught me in childhood, which had dropped away from me of itself when my mind had matured. The more I studied, the more I was convinced that truth could not be there...

I could not return to the faith of my childhood, nor could I believe in any of the faiths professed by other nations, for in all of them there were the same contradictions, absurdities, miracles, denials of all other faiths, and above all the same dishonest demand for blind confidence in their teaching.

So I became convinced that I should not find an answer to my question and the alleviation of my sufferings among the existing faiths, and my despair was so great that I contemplated suicide.

But then I came upon my salvation. And this salvation resulted from the fact that from childhood I had retained a dim idea that the Gospels contain a reply to my question. In their teaching – despite the perversions to which it is subjected by the doctrine of the Christian Church – I scented the truth. And I made a last attempt to solve the problem. Putting aside all interpretations, I began to read and study the Gospels and penetrate into their meaning. And the more I penetrated into their meaning the more something new manifested itself to me, quite unlike the teaching of the Christian Church, but which answered my question. And at last that reply became perfectly plain.

And that reply was not merely plain but indubitable, first because it fully coincided with the demands of my heart and my reason, and secondly because when I understood it I saw that it was not my exclusive explanation of the Gospel, as might at first appear, nor was it an exclusive revelation of Christ's, but that it was the same reply to life's question that has been given more or less clearly by all the best representatives of humanity both before and since the Gospels – beginning with Moses, Isaiah, Confucius, the ancient Greeks, Buddha, Socrates, and down to Pascal, Spinoza, Fichte, Feuerbach, and those others – often unnoticed and undistinguished men – who without accepting any creed or faith, have sincerely thought and spoken of the meaning of life. So that in the knowledge of truth that I gathered from the Gospels, not only was I not alone, but I was in the company of all the best men of former and present times. And I became assured of this truth and was reassured, and have joyfully lived twenty years of my life since then and am now joyfully approaching my death.

Leo Tolstoy, from Preface to The Christian Teaching, in Vol. 12 of his Works, OUP, 1934

Let us pray

Our prayer, written by Bishop Westcott at the same time that Tolstoy was writing, was intended for use before bible study.

Blessed Lord, by whose providence all holy scriptures were written and preserved for our instruction, give us grace to study them this and every day with patience and love. Strengthen our souls with the fulness of their divine teaching. Keep from us all pride and irreverence. Guide us in the deep things of thy heavenly wisdom, and of thy great mercy lead us by thy Word unto everlasting life; through Jesus Christ our Lord and Saviour.

May the blessing of God almighty, the Father, the Son, and the Holy Spirit, be with us and remain with us this day and for ever. *Amen.*

NOTES ON ASSEMBLIES 29–31

1. *The remaining four of seven assemblies*

Assemblies 29–31 are part of an introduction to the reading of the Sermon on the Mount. The fourth (Friday's) assembly consisted of a recording of a BBC ten-to-eight talk, an interview with a West African missionary who was home on furlough, the Reverend Kennedy Thom (January 1968). This talk admirably completed the week's readings and prepared the way for the gospel, thus:

Last week we looked at various reactions to the challenge of the Christian gospel:
– the symbolic interpretations of the Middle Ages,
– the historical criticism of this century,
– the personal response of Tolstoy,
– the response in action of a modern missionary.
For Tolstoy, the kernel of the gospel is in the Sermon on the Mount, and many of you would say the same thing.
The Sermon on the Mount: We talk about it, and hear it talked about, but how many of us have read it?
We shall hear it this week. It comes in Chapters 5, 6, and 7 of St Matthew's gospel, and we shall hear Chapter 5 today, Chapter 6 tomorrow, and Chapter 7 on Wednesday. Try to listen to it as if you had not heard it before. And to give it some freshness we shall hear it in a recent translation: J. B. Phillips'.

I found that Sixth Formers could hear the Sermon on the Mount read in this way. The reading had to be well done, in this case by the Senior Chemistry master. Long bible passages made a welcome variety in texture of assemblies after the previous week's introduction.

2. Variety of approach to the life and teaching of Jesus Christ is essential if school worship is not merely to grind out once again an oft-told tale. In *Sixth Form Worship*, three approaches based on books are described; on T. R. Glover, *The Jesus of History*; on Gilbert Highet, *The Art of Teaching*; on Lord Eccles, *Half-way to Faith*. In Assemblies 38–40 we outline an approach which could involve student research. Obviously these several approaches would not all be used in the same term.

3. To offset the Tolstoy passage, the story of Charles Darwin's religion might be read, though its direction is different. Darwin recognized in later life that his love of poetry atrophied because, in his busy scientific work, he gave no time to poetry, so that when he returned to it, hoping to enjoy it, the appetite had gone. His religious change of attitude sprang from a similar erosion, though others might come to the same conclusion after much spiritual distress. See *The Autobiography of Charles Darwin*, Collins, 1958, pp. 85 f.

Assembly 32 (1 of 6)

Ezekiel: The Background of the Law

Used at the beginning of the Autumn term

Leader

I want to welcome the new First Year Sixth to our Sixth Form assembly. We do not sing hymns (as you did in the Main School assembly) – mostly we speak and think.

> I hope, *think*; because assembly should help us
>> to widen our sympathies and understanding,
>> to know ourselves,
>> to find a basis for living.

As humans we do not only experience things, but we reflect on our experience. Without such reflection we can never attain wisdom.

Today we shall hear a passage which will mean more and more as you use your imagination. It comes from an arid book in the bible, the book of *Leviticus*, a book of rules and regulations. It ends with a saying you know.

Some of you will be aware that masters talk of 'writing Leviticus', or adding a chapter to Leviticus, when they work out school rules. Our rules, or regulations, are meant to codify acceptable practice.

But the passage gets beyond rules to a genuine caring for others. You've got to *care* to see why some of the rules are there.

Reading

And the Lord said to Moses, 'Say to all the congregation of the people of Israel, When you reap the harvest of your land, you shall not reap your field to its very border, neither shall you gather the gleanings after your harvest. And you shall not strip your vineyard bare, neither shall you gather the fallen grapes of your vineyard; you shall leave them for the poor and for the sojourner: I am the Lord your God.

'You shall not steal, nor deal falsely, nor lie to one another: I am the Lord.

'You shall not oppress your neighbour or rob him. The wages of a hired servant shall not remain with you all night until the morning.

You shall not curse the deaf or put a stumbling block before the blind, but you shall fear your God: I am the Lord.

'You shall do no injustice in judgment; you shall not be partial to the poor or defer to the great, but in righteousness shall you judge your neighbour. You shall not go up and down as a slanderer among your people (or, as the Authorized Version has it: as a talebearer), and you shall not stand forth against the life of your neighbour: I am the Lord.

'You shall not hate your brother in your heart, but you shall reason with your neighbour, lest you bear sin because of him. You shall not take vengeance or bear any grudge against the sons of your own people, but you shall love your neighbour as yourself: I am the Lord.'

Lev. 19. 1, 2a, 9–11, 12b, 13–18 *RSV*

Leader

'You shall love your neighbour as yourself' – so you've got to love yourself? Well, yes. What that means must wait. And you've got to love your neighbour, too.

May I end with a definition of such love, free of all sentimentality: it involves *thinking* and caring (it is from C. F. Andrews):

> *Love is the accurate estimate and supply of someone else's need.*

Let us pray

(The prayer was written a long time ago by a headmaster of the Leys School in Cambridge for use in his school.)

O heavenly Father, who hast taught us that all our gifts without charity are nothing worth, shed abroad that most excellent gift in our hearts. Grant that, while we enjoy the things that we possess, we ourselves may never be possessed by them. May our own hearts ever be touched with the feeling of others' necessities, that we may be quick in sympathy and ready in helpfulness. In our inmost thought of life redeem us from pride and from selfishness; and evermore inspire us, as wise and compassionate stewards of our great heritage, freely to share with others thy manifold gifts of love to us; through Jesus Christ our Lord.

H. Bisseker

The Lord's Prayer

All The grace of our Lord Jesus Christ,
and the love of God,
and the fellowship of the Holy Spirit,
be with us all evermore. Amen.

Ezekiel's Vision

A picture, a colour print of the head of Ezekiel, from Michelangelo's fresco in the Sistine Chapel, was on view.

Leader

Yesterday we heard the passage which ends, 'You shall love your neighbour as yourself', and we referred to that very unromantic definition of love: Love is the accurate estimate and supply of someone else's need.

Love your neighbour as yourself: then you must love yourself? How, in this sense? . . . accurately estimating yourself.

It cuts out the frivolous attitude which never takes anything seriously. It means abandoning fantasy ideas about ourselves; we have to learn to accept our own personalities and powers. It means being responsible for our own future, for our own growth, realizing that what we are and do now affects what we shall become.

This sounds far more serious than it really is; being realistic about one's self, being self-aware, does not cut out joy. 'The accurate estimate of oneself' – Is that possible for us?

On the wall is EZEKIEL – part of a picture in the Sistine Chapel in Rome, painted by Michelangelo – Ezekiel, the Old Testament prophet. He was called of God and abased himself. But he had to stand on his feet, he had to be himself, without false modesty, before God could use him.

We shall hear the story of his vision and call. It might have been the hallucinatory vision of a drug addict. But drugs make you morally limp. His call was to effective action.

Reading

It was in the thirtieth year, on the fifth day of the fourth month, as I was among the exiles at the river Kebar, that heaven opened and I saw visions of God. The hand of the Eternal was on me in a trance, and as I gazed, there was a storm-wind blowing from the north! – a huge cloud with fire flashing out of it, and with a sheen encircling it and issuing from it, the colour of amber. Out of it appeared the forms of four Creatures, and this was their appearance: they had the same form, each with four faces and four wings, with limbs straight and gleaming like burnished bronze, and with the soles of their feet rounded like the feet of calves, Under their wings, on the four sides of them, were human hands. As for their four faces and wings – their wings touched one another, and their faces never turned as they moved; each moved straight forward. As for the likeness of their faces – all four had in front the face of a man, on the right the face of a lion, on the left the face of a bull, and the face of an eagle at the back. Their wings were stretched out, one pair to touch the next Creature, the other pair to cover the body. Each moved straight forward; wherever the Spirit impelled them to go they went, never turning as they moved. Also, in the middle of the Creatures there was Something moving to and fro, like glowing coals, like torches, a fire that gleamed and flashed out lightning.

Above the vault over their heads was the semblance of a throne, blue like a sapphire, and on the throne-like appearance there was the semblance of a human form; from the waist upwards I saw Something glowing like amber or fire, from the waist downwards there was Something resembling fire, while all around there was a bright halo like the rainbow that appears in the clouds after rain. Such was the appearance of what resembled the Splendour of the Eternal.

When I saw it, I fell on my face; then I heard the voice of one speaking.

He said to me, 'Son of man, stand up and I will speak to you.' As he spoke, the Spirit entered me and made me stand upon my feet. I heard him address me. 'Son of man,' he said, 'I am sending you to the Israelites, to a rebellious race who have rebelled against me; they and their fathers have sinned against me down to this day. I am sending you to them, impudent and obstinate as they are, and you must tell them what the Eternal says.'

Ezek. 1. 1, 3b–14, 25–28; 2. 1–4 *Moffatt*

Leader

Do you get the meaning of that? Of the Spirit entering Ezekiel and making him stand on his feet?

Love is the accurate estimate and supply of someone else's need. Is it possible to have an accurate estimate of yourself, neither to belittle yourself, nor to over-rate yourself, but to stand on your feet? I think so. And you must love your neighbour *as yourself*.

Let us pray

O God, who workest all things, who hast called us to be fellow workers with thee, and dost assign to every man his separate task: Teach us, in our several callings, what thou wouldst have us do, and make us faithful to do it, in thy Name and in thy strength; for Jesus Christ's sake.

From Milner-White & Briggs, *Daily Prayer*,
OUP, 1941

Assembly 34 (3 of 6)

Ezekiel: A Message of Hope

Leader

At our last assembly we heard part of the account of Ezekiel's vision and of his call:

> Son of man, stand upon your feet, and I will speak with you.

And later:

> Son of man, I have made you a watchman for the house of Israel. (3. 17, *RSV*)

For over twenty years Ezekiel prophesied – that is, he spoke the word of God as it came to him in vision and in thought. (The word *prophecy* in the Old Testament, you will know, does not mean a cheap foretelling of the future; it refers to compulsive utterances in the name of the Lord.)

Ezekiel's was a thankless and difficult task. Michelangelo's picture catches some of his intensity. He wrote down what he had to say, and some of his forty-eight chapters are of great literary merit. We shall hear from three of them during this week.

First, the background:

Ezekiel was deported from Jerusalem to Babylon with the first convoy of exiles in 597 BC at about the age of twenty-five. He was about thirty when the call came to him. Some years later, in 586, Jerusalem fell – the whole nation was in exile.

Babylon exercised a fascination on the Hebrews. Though not badly treated, they were robbed of home and country; they might easily have been absorbed, losing nationality, and religion too. It was the prophets and singers of the Exile who kept hope and faith alive.

Ezekiel's message falls into three parts:

1. Before the fall of Jerusalem: warning.
    If the people persist in forsaking the ways of righteousness, judgment will certainly fall.
2. After the fall: hope.
    God will yet save his people.

3. The last chapters:
   a description of what the restored commonwealth of Israel will be like when worship is centred in a new Temple at Jerusalem.

Today we shall hear the most famous passage from the book, from the middle section. A message of hope. Applicable to any who are suffering from disappointment, having failed; any captive or persecuted people. The style is typical: a vision, told in a literary style which is readily translatable, so that even in translation it is powerfully emotional.

Reading

The hand of the Lord was upon me, and he brought me out by the Spirit of the Lord, and set me down in the midst of the valley; it was full of bones. And he led me round among them; and behold, there were very many upon the valley; and lo, they were very dry. And he said to me, 'Son of man, can these bones live?' And I answered, 'O Lord God, thou knowest.' Again he said to me, 'Prophesy to these bones, and say to them, O dry bones, hear the word of the Lord. Thus says the Lord God to these bones: Behold, I will cause breath to enter you, and you shall live. And I will lay sinews upon you, and will cause flesh to come upon you, and cover you with skin, and put breath in you, and you shall live; and you shall know that I am the Lord.'

So I prophesied as I was commanded; and as I prophesied, there was a noise, and behold, a rattling; and the bones came together, bone to its bone. And as I looked, there were sinews on them, and flesh had come upon them, and skin had covered them; but there was no breath in them. Then he said to me, 'Prophesy to the breath, prophesy, son of man, and say to the breath, Thus says the Lord God: Come from the four winds, O breath, and breathe upon these slain, that they may live.' So I prophesied as he commanded me, and the breath came into them, and they lived, and stood upon their feet, an exceeding great host.

Then he said to me, 'Son of man, these bones are the whole house of Israel. Behold, they say, 'Our bones are dried up, and our hope is lost; we are clean cut off.' Therefore prophesy, and say to them, Thus says the Lord God: Behold, I will open your graves, and raise you from your graves, O my people; and I will bring you home into the land of Israel. And you shall know that I am the Lord, when I open your graves, and raise you from your graves, O my people. And I will put my Spirit within you, and you shall live, and I will place you in your own land; then you shall know that I, the Lord, have spoken, and I have done it, says the Lord.'

Ezek. 37. 1–14 *RSV*

Let us pray

(In our prayer we shall hear first a short passage from Ezekiel, then a prayer about the changelessness of God; finally we shall say together the Grace.)

I will give them one heart, and put a new spirit within them; I will take the stony heart out of their flesh and give them a heart of flesh, that they may walk in my statutes and keep my ordinances and obey them; and they shall be my people, and I will be their God.

Ezek. 11. 19–20

Eternal God, who changest not, as men change; who, though we be faithless, yet abidest faithful: Increase both our faith in the unchanging love of thy purpose, and our steadfastness in the doing of thy will; for Jesus Christ's sake.

From Milner-White & Briggs, *Daily Prayer*, OUP, 1941

All The grace of our Lord Jesus Christ,
and the love of God,
and the fellowship of the Holy Spirit,
be with us all evermore.   Amen.

Ezekiel: Woe to the Shepherds

Leader

Ezekiel was a watchman for Israel – warning of danger, explaining the reason for suffering.

Why the failure of Israel? Why the convoys of exiles to Babylon? Two reasons: the leaders of Israel had failed to do justice, and the people themselves had failed.

In our second reading from the prophecy we shall hear of the shepherds of Israel – the kings and leaders – who had betrayed their trust.

First Reading

This word from the Eternal also came to me: 'Son of man, prophesy against the rulers of Israel, prophesy thus to these shepherds: "Here is what the Lord the Eternal says: Woe to the shepherds of Israel who have fed none but themselves! Ought not shepherds to feed their flock? You have seized the milk, you have clothed yourselves with the wool, you have killed the fatlings, but you have not fed the flock. You never put strength into the weak, you never healed the sickly, you never bandaged the cripples, you never recovered those who had been driven away, you never looked for those who were lost, and you were rough to those who were strong. So my flock has been scattered because they had no shepherd, and it has been devoured by all the wild beasts. My flock strayed all over the uplands and over every high hill, scattered all over the face of the earth, with none to search for them, none to look after them." Hear, then, what the Eternal has to say to you shepherds. "By my life!" says the Lord the Eternal, "since my flock has become the prey and food of every wild animal, because there was no one to shepherd them (for the shepherds cared nothing about my flock, but fed themselves instead of feeding my flock)" – hear then what the Lord the Eternal says, you shepherds – "I am against the shepherds, I will demand my flock back from them, I will stop them from attending my flock; no longer shall the shepherds feed themselves, I will rescue my flock from their greed, and no longer shall it be food for them." For this is what the Lord the Eternal says: "I myself, I will search for my flock and look for them. As a shepherd looks for his flock on the day when his sheep have been scattered, so will I search for my flock and bring them safe from all the places whither they have been scattered on a day of clouds and darkness: I myself will tend my flock, I will take them to their pasture," says the Lord the Eternal.'

Ezek. 34. 1–12, 15 Moffatt

Leader

In the seventeenth century many thought the 'shepherds' were the religious leaders, the priests. Milton drew on this passage when, in *Lycidas*, he foretold the ruin of the corrupted clergy.

Second Reading

> Blind mouthes! that scarce themselves know how to hold
> A Sheep-hook, or have learn'd ought els the least
> That to the faithfull Herdmans art belongs!
> What recks it them? What need they? They are sped;
> And when they list, their lean and flashy songs
> Grate on their scrannel Pipes of wretched straw,
> The hungry Sheep look up, and are not fed,
> But swoln with wind, and the rank mist they draw,
> Rot inwardly, and foul contagion spread:
> Besides what the grim Woolf with privy paw
> Daily devours apace, and nothing sed,
> But that two-handed engine at the door,
> Stands ready to smite once, and smite no more.

Lycidas, lines 119–131

Leader

And what does all this mean?

Do you remember Alice talking to the Duchess in *Alice in Wonderland*? – You should read it. The Duchess is speaking:

'I can't tell you just now what the moral of that is, but I shall remember it in a bit.'

'Perhaps it hasn't one,' Alice ventured to remark.

'Tut, tut, child!' said the Duchess. 'Everything's got a moral, if only you can find it.'

And the moral of our story is this:

If you are in a school, holding an office, taking a place . . . you have a job to do. If you fail, you not only fail yourself – you fail others who look up to you, and you obstruct others who would have done the job properly.

He's a grim chap, is Ezekiel, isn't he?

Let us pray

Grant to us, O God, this day to do whatever duty lies before us with cheerfulness and sincerity of heart. Help us in all things fearlessly to do what we know is right. Remove from us all hypocrisy and pretence. Make us truthful, unselfish, and strong. And so bring us to the ending of the day unashamed and with a quiet mind; through Jesus Christ our Lord.

Uppingham Prayer-Book

Ezekiel: A Call to Righteousness

Leader

Negro spirituals were songs that gave spirit to a slave people; they sprang from faith. Nowadays they are often deemed entertainment – words without meaning.

That is what Ezekiel feared for his message.

Grim it sounded yesterday. But people were attracted by his voice, his dramatic gifts, his denunciatory style; he was an artist! It began to be the fashion to go to hear him; a kind of conventional collective masochism.

This is what he said, speaking of himself:

> Lo, thou art unto them as a very lovely song of one that hath a pleasant voice, and can play well on an instrument: for they hear thy words, but they do them not.
>
> *Ezek*. 33. 32 *AV*

What was his message? Put impersonally it was this:

Goodness has the universe on its side. The only *viable* way of life is to follow righteousness.

The world is so governed that evil is self-frustrating, self-defeating; its rewards are short-lived. To sin is to seal your own death; it is suicide.

To do good is to live. It is to grow, to become yourself, to find integrity.

The world is a moral world, so structured that only what is just is, in the end, viable. You neglect this at your peril.

But Ezekiel made all this personal. No good blaming your heredity, your fathers. What matters is *your* choice. The parable of the sour grapes is a telling one. *You* eat sour grapes; *your* teeth are set on edge. Don't blame others.

We shall hear part of Chapter 18, emphasizing the logic of this almost impersonal justice.

Reading

The word of the Lord came to me again: 'What do you mean by repeating this proverb concerning the land of Israel, "The fathers have eaten sour grapes, and the children's teeth are set on edge"? As I live, says the Lord God, this proverb shall be no more used by you in Israel. Behold, all souls are mine; the soul of the father as well as the soul of the son is mine: the soul that sins shall die.

'If a man is righteous and does what is lawful and right – if he does not eat upon the mountains or lift up his eyes to the idols of the house of Israel, does not oppress anyone, but restores to the debtor his pledge, commits no robbery, gives his bread to the hungry and covers the naked with a garment, does not lend at interest or take any increase, withholds his hand from iniquity, executes true justice between man and man, walks in my statutes, and is careful to observe my ordinances – he is righteous, he shall surely live, says the Lord God.

'The soul that sins shall die. The son shall not suffer for the iniquity of the father, nor the father suffer for the iniquity of the son; the righteousness of the righteous shall be upon himself, and the wickedness of the wicked shall be upon himself.

'But if a wicked man turns away from all his sins which he has committed and keeps all my statutes and does what is lawful and right, he shall surely live; he shall not die. None of the transgressions which he has committed shall be remembered against him; for the righteousness which he has done he shall live. Have I any pleasure in the death of the wicked, says the Lord God, and not rather that he should turn from his way and live? But when a righteous man turns away from his righteousness and commits iniquity and does the same abominable things that the wicked man does, shall he live? None of the righteous deeds which he has done shall be remembered; for the treachery of which he is guilty and the sin he has committed, he shall die.

'Yet you say, "The way of the Lord is not just." Hear now, O house of Israel: Is my way not just? Is it not your ways that are not just? When a righteous man turns away from his righteousness and commits iniquity, he shall die for it; for the iniquity which he has committed he shall die. Again, when a wicked man turns away from the wickedness he has committed and does what is lawful and right, he shall save his life. Because he considered and turned away from all the transgressions which he has committed, he shall surely live, he shall not die. Yet the house of Israel says, "The way of the Lord is not just." O house of Israel, are my ways not just? Is it not your ways that are not just?

'Therefore I will judge you, O house of Israel, every one according to his ways, says the Lord God. Repent and turn from all your transgressions, lest iniquity be your ruin. Cast away from you all the transgressions which you have committed against me, and get yourselves a new heart and a new spirit! Why will you die, O house of Israel? For I have no pleasure in the death of anyone, says the Lord God; so turn, and live.'

Ezek. 18. 1–6a, 7–9, 20–32 *RSV*

Let us pray

O God and Father of all, who hast shown unto man light and darkness, right and wrong, that he may choose freely between them: Grant us both generosity and courage to choose the good and to refuse the evil, that we may be numbered among thy sons in whom thou art well-pleased, and who dwell in thy presence, through Jesus Christ our Lord.

From Milner-White & Briggs, *Daily Prayer*,
OUP, 1941
Modified by permission

Ezekiel: Dry Bones: A Dramatized Scene

Narrator
Ezekiel
The Shepherd
The Vulture

The People ⎫ *voices remembered*
The Soldiers ⎭ *by Ezekiel*

Narrator Ezekiel's message to the people changed from condemnation to comfort. The dark days of your captivity will come to an end, he says. God will gather you together and bring you back to your own land. He will look after you as a shepherd looks after his sheep. No one will harm you any more.

When Ezekiel made these promises the Jews were still in captivity. There seemed little hope of escape. Promises were all right. But how were they to be fulfilled? Many of the captives had been in Babylon for a long time. Some of them, perhaps, had given up hope of ever seeing Jerusalem again. Only a miracle could save them. And very few believed at that time that the miracle would happen. What a difficult job Ezekiel had to convince them.

However, he tries again, telling of another strange vision which came to him.

Ezekiel is alone in the desert, a day's march from the city.

Ezekiel What is it that the Lord requires of me?
What is it I seek? I have come out of the city
A day's march, led by the word of the Lord,
Lifted as it were by the hair of the head, carried by the breath of the Lord;
The sun is hot on the desert. There is no water;
No water in the desert. There is no shade.
Not even a little shade under a rock.
There is no life here. Not a green leaf,
Not a blade of grass, not even a lizard
Or a snake hiding under a stone. Stones underfoot,
And the hot dry sand, and rocks that burn the hand.
There is nothing here. I must sit down and drink
The last water from my flask. What does the Lord want of me?

I do not know why I have come to this place.
What is it I am seeking?

The Vulture No life in the desert, Ezekiel?
Look up! *I* am alive. I am here, above you, here in the hot sky,
A speck you can hardly see in the hot blue sky.
Riding high in the sky, turning and wheeling and watching
For life so that I may strike like a stone falling.
I am biding my time, Ezekiel. Biding my time.

Ezekiel (*shuddering*) I had not seen the vulture overhead,
Biding its time. But now that I look,
I have been here before.
Surely I have seen this place; the jagged rocks,
The stony pathway, and those two outcropping hills –
We came this way to Babylon.

The Voices of the People (*repeating as in a dream the words of their march*)

Another night and another day.
We are tired. We are thirsty.
How many miles to Babylon?
How much further to go?

The Voices of the Soldiers Hurry along there. Hurry along.
There is no water in the desert.
If you can't keep up you will die in the desert,
And your bones will grow white in the sun,
Like those dry bones over there,
Picked clean by the vultures.

Ezekiel (*standing to look*)

The vultures! . . . I had forgotten.
I thought that those were white stones over yonder.
I see now that they are bones; dry dead bones
Whitened by the sun; bones that once were men;
Unburied, dry, dry, parched and bleached and dead in the desert,
In the valley of death. . . . The valley of the shadow of death.
'Even though I walk through the valley of the shadow of death
I will fear no evil –'

The Vulture (*interrupting forcefully*)

Do you fear *no* evil, Ezekiel?
Do you not fear the desert and the dead men's bones,

And the black speck riding in the sky, biding its time?
Ezekiel (*loudly*) 'I will fear no evil.
Thy rod and thy staff they comfort me . . .'
Is that a man under the rock, in a little patch of shade
I had not seen before? It is a man.
He has a shepherd's staff in his hand. Where can he feed his sheep
In this place? He should lead them in green pastures.
The Shepherd Come here, Ezekiel.
Ezekiel Sir, I am here.
The Shepherd You see these bones.
Son of man, can these bones live?
Ezekiel Sir, thou knowest.
The Shepherd Prophesy to these bones, and say to them
'O dry bones, hear the word of the Lord!'
Thus says the Lord God to these bones,
'Behold, I will cause breath to enter you,
And you shall live. I will lay sinews upon you,
And will cause flesh to come upon these bones,
And cover you with skin, and you shall live;
And you shall know that I am the Lord.'
Prophesy to the bones, Ezekiel.
Ezekiel (*with a loud cry*) O dry bones, hear the word of the Lord!
The Shepherd What do you hear, Ezekiel?
Ezekiel (*covering his eyes, afraid*) I hear a noise . . . A rattling,
Rustling like dry leaves, bones coming together.
Bone to its bone. Bone to its bone.
The Shepherd Look at them now!
Ezekiel (*drawing a deep breath*) Flesh has come upon them. Skin has covered them.
But there is no breath in them. They lie there still in the sun.
The Shepherd Prophesy to the wind. Prophesy, son of man;
Say to the wind, 'Thus saith the Lord God;
Come from the four winds, O breath, and breathe upon the slain
That they may live.'
Ezekiel (*covering his eyes*) O wind; O breath; O spirit of the Lord;
Breathe on these bones.
The Shepherd (*after a moment, quietly*) What do you see, Ezekiel?
Ezekiel (*looks for several moments, then speaks, awed*) The breath has come upon them.
Their eyes are open. They move, and turn,

And rise on their knees, and stand upon their feet.
They are alive, an army of men and women;
An exceeding great host, host upon host.
Sir, who are they?

The Shepherd Son of man, these bones are the whole house of Israel.
They say, 'Behold our bones are dried up,
Our hope is lost, and we are clean cut off.'
Therefore prophesy to them; say to the house of Israel,
'Thus says the Lord, "Behold, my people,
I will open your graves, and raise you from your graves,
And I will bring you home into the land of Israel.
And you shall know, when I open your graves,
That I am the Lord. And I will give you my Spirit
And you shall live, and you shall know that I
The Lord have spoken. And I have done this," says the Lord.'

Ezekiel bows his head to the ground. When he looks up the Shepherd has gone. He rises slowly to his feet and looks around him.

Ezekiel The valley is quiet and empty under the sun.
Where is the Shepherd? . . . There is nothing.
Even the vultures have gone. There is nothing under the rock where he stood
But the shadow of the great rock, and a faint sound as of water;
Can it be water in the desert?
A little trickle of water, and a handful of green blades
In the cleft of the rock. New life in the desert.
I will fill my flask again,
I will go back to Babylon, to the green pastures
And the still waters, where he leadeth me.
'Surely goodness and mercy shall follow me all the days of my life.'
Surely life comes out of the hand of the Lord . . .
Surely the breath of the Lord shall come into these dry bones,
And his people shall live.

Let us pray

First, a prayer; then an act of praise.

A prayer. Come, thou Holy Spirit, restore the lives which, without thee, are as dead; kindle the hearts which, without thee, are cold and dull; enlighten the minds which, without thee, are blind and dark.

An act of praise. O Holy Spirit of life, who fillest all the world, we worship and adore thee. Spirit of light, who teachest all truth, we worship and adore thee. Source of all gifts of nature and of grace, of knowledge natural and supernatural, we worship and adore thee. For that thou hast made and endowed us, taught and reproved us, borne with us, recovered us, restored us; Lord and lifegiver, we worship and adore thee.

From *A Book of Prayers for Everyman*, SPCK

And now commitment: May the Spirit, O God, which proceeds from thee, illuminate our minds and lead us into all truth; through Jesus Christ our Lord. Amen.

NOTES ON ASSEMBLIES 32–37

1. *The occasion*

These assemblies were first used at the beginning of a school year. There had already been the initial full school assembly; now, for the first time, the new Sixth Form entrants were taking part in separate Sixth Form worship. Assembly 32 does not give all the reasons for worship; it was intended to set the tone, and to be an introduction to the general talk that followed – about the Sixth Former's place in the school (volunteer now, not conscript), the need for positive choices (of courses, for instance, and how to get guidance), the opportunities provided (including Voluntary Service), and so on.

2. *The C. F. Andrews definition*

I found this in Simon Phipps, *God on Monday* (Hodder & Stoughton, 1966), a useful little book in other ways too.

3. *The Michelangelo print*

This was on view for all the Assemblies 33–36. The print area of the big head is $11'' \times 14\frac{1}{2}''$, well worth getting.

4. *Treatment*

Assembly is not the place for Old Testament history – just enough to make the readings relevant for today. Since we developed this style for the Sixth Form, similar developments have taken place in the Main School. Rarely is a bible passage read without some introduction or comment.

5. *The dramatized scene*

This was written by my wife, Morwenna Bielby, for *Two Refugees: Ezekiel & Second Isaiah* (D. S. Russell & M. R. Bielby, SCM Press,

1962), a book designed for the years before school leaving (14–15), and containing many similar dramatized scenes. Nevertheless the Sixth Form enjoyed it; the Senior English master played the Vulture, the Drama master Ezekiel.

6. *Other prophets*

This treatment should not be too soon repeated. Micah, however, provides useful pegs: 'What does the Lord require of you but to do justice (your duty to all men), and to love kindness (your duty to those near to you), and to walk humbly with your God (your duty to yourself)' (*Micah* 6. 8).

Assembly 38 (1 of 3)

The Four Evangelists · 1

Leader

Christianity is full of symbols; so are most religions and, indeed, so is ordinary life. The lion is a symbol of courage, the mouse of timidity, the owl of wisdom. In Christian art and architecture you find the dove, the lamb, the lily; monograms too, IHS, the chi-rho, alpha and omega.

During this week we shall consider symbols of the four evangelists, the writers of the gospels. You find them on the covers of the Pelican Gospel Commentaries, and as headings in the translation (by E. V. Rieu) of the gospels in the Penguin Classics series: they are heraldic figures. They come from the earliest days of Christianity, and decorate early manuscripts, and find a place in many churches:

>for Matthew: the winged man,
>for Mark: the winged lion,
>for Luke: the winged ox,
>for John: the winged eagle.

The origin of these symbols is in the book of *Revelation*, a book which draws largely on the literary symbols of the Old Testament, and especially on the account of Ezekiel's vision. Hear, then, part of John's description of heaven from the *Revelation*.

Reading

In the centre, round the throne itself, were four living creatures, covered with eyes, in front and behind. The first creature was like a lion, the second like an ox, the third had a human face, the fourth was like an eagle in flight. The four living creatures, each of them with six wings, had eyes all over, inside and out; and by day and by night without a pause they sang:

'Holy, holy, holy is God the sovereign Lord of all, who was, and is, and is to come!'

As often as the living creatures give glory and honour and thanks to the One who sits on the throne, who lives for ever and ever, the twenty-four elders fall down before the One who sits on the throne and worship him who lives for ever and ever; and as they lay their crowns before the throne they cry:

'Thou art worthy, O Lord our God, to receive glory and honour and power, because thou didst create all things; by thy will they were created, and have their being!'

Rev. 4. 6b–11 *NEB*

Leader

There is nothing there about the four gospels; but there *are* four living creatures. And is not four the number of universality – there are four points of the compass – and is not the gospel for all men? That may not be a valid argument, but it is the kind of argument used by Irenaeus in the second half of the second century. Irenaeus was an émigré from Asia Minor to Gaul; he became bishop of Lyons. 'There must be four gospels', he said, 'just as there were four faces in the vision of Ezekiel, those of a man, a lion, an ox, and an eagle.' And so the symbolic representation began. Biblical scholars may regret it – it neither helps in the understanding of *Ezekiel* or the *Revelation*, nor is it easy to justify – but it has become the starting point of much artistic invention.

During this week we shall examine the association of these winged figures with the evangelists, and see, also, how they are used in local churches.

Let us pray

O God, we are glad that truth comes to us in many ways; that factual statements, scientific laws and verbal propositions are not the only kind of truth.

We are glad we have hearts and souls as well as brains, and that truth embraces feeling and attitude as well as intellect.

Teach us to value all the ways in which man communicates with man, and all the ways in which your truth for life is waiting for our understanding.

So help us to see beyond the outward, beyond the sign and symbol, to that which these things convey, to that which they have meant for many generations.

May we value our heritage and learn from it, even when it speaks in a language which we cannot now use, through Jesus Christ our Lord.

Grant us, O Lord, honesty in our thinking, sincerity in our feelings, integrity in our relations with others, and truth in all things. *Amen.*

The Four Evangelists · 2

Leader

The eagle, soaring to heaven, is the symbol of inspiration. That is why lecterns, in many churches, have the shape of an eagle. Of the four gospels, John's stands out, different from the others; it is the product of much reflection on the significance of the coming of Jesus. Some call it 'the spiritual gospel'. And so it is the eagle, of the four living creatures of the Apocalypse, which has been taken as the symbol of this gospel.

I am going to ask one of the group that has been looking at local churches to report.

A Student

We have looked at seven churches in Huddersfield and we found that four of them have the symbols of the writers of the gospels. The easiest to see are in the east window of St Paul's Church at Armitage Bridge. Apparently this window used to be completely of coloured glass, but most of this has been removed and now there are just four coloured panels in otherwise plain glass. These show the winged creatures, each with a scroll; the winged man, St Matthew; the lion, St Mark; the ox, St Luke; and the eagle, St John.

In the oldest church in Huddersfield, Almondbury parish church, we found elaborate carved figures and panels behind the altar, painted in bright colours. Four of the figures are angels carrying shields, and on these, in gold, are the four symbolic figures.

But we found that the church which is richest in symbols is Emmanuel, at Lockwood. The altar cross contains the figures which represent the gospel writers, at the four extremities, with the eagle at the top and the winged man at the bottom. The cross also has on it the chi-rho, the alpha and omega, and a Latin inscription.

We discovered that the school is in the parish of Lindley, so we looked carefully at Lindley parish church, and, in the end, we found the four symbols we were looking for, high up, in the rose window at the east end of the church. They are not very easily seen.

Leader

Thank you; no doubt many of you will want to see these churches and, perhaps, look for other symbols and their meanings. For today, let us think of St John's gospel, represented by the eagle, the topmost figure on the altar cross in the Lockwood parish church.

How does St John soar? He sees meanings in incidents which we might regard as ordinary – and so the ordinary, itself, becomes a symbol of another sort. We shall hear his account of one incident; the thing to note is the juxtaposition of the self-awareness of Jesus and the task he performs – an illustration of what John meant when, in his preface to the gospel, he said 'the Word became flesh'.

Reading

During supper, Jesus, well aware that the Father had entrusted everything to him, and that he had come from God and was going back to God, rose from table, laid aside his garments, and taking a towel, tied it round him. Then he poured water into a basin, and began to wash his disciples' feet and to wipe them with the towel.

When it was Simon Peter's turn, Peter said to him, 'You, Lord, washing my feet?' Jesus replied, 'You do not understand now what I am doing, but one day you will.' Peter said, 'I will never let you wash my feet.' 'If I do not wash you,' Jesus replied, 'you are not in fellowship with me.' 'Then, Lord,' said Simon Peter, 'not my feet only; wash my hands and head as well!'

Jesus said, 'A man who has bathed needs no further washing; he is altogether clean.'

John 13. 3–10a *NEB*

Let us pray

O God, we are glad there is mystery for us still to explore – there is wonder in your dealings with man.

We are glad for the Johns of this world, men whose spirits soar like the eagle, who themselves see your ways in ordinary life and who challenge us to understand your revelation aright.

Help us never to belittle the past, for its records include the story of Jesus. Help us never to ignore the future, for we are moving into it, and what we are and do partly determine it. Help us to see in our present – our successes and failures in our contacts with others, our ability or inability to recognize and meet our own deeper needs – help us, in these things, to see your way for us.

So may we, in our turn, know something of the inwardness of your speaking to and through the spirit of man.

All   And may the grace of our Lord Jesus Christ,
and the love of God,
and the fellowship of the Holy Spirit,
be with us all evermore.   Amen.

The Four Evangelists · 3

Leader

The winged man, the winged lion, and the winged ox remain: Matthew, Mark, Luke. How did this association come about? What characteristics of the gospels explain it?

We, ourselves, speak of the three synoptic gospels; they tell the story of the ministry of Jesus in much the same way, each having its special emphasis. It is John, the eagle, who soars, though some find his style too polemical.

As a matter of fact, the association, the winged man with Matthew, the lion with Mark, the ox with Luke, is largely conventional. Irenaeus, who in the second century first brought together these winged creatures and the gospels, made a different linking. For him John was the lion and Mark the eagle. These two had been exchanged by the fifth century when the use of the symbols in art appears for the first time. Since then, the association we now know has been unchanged.

Most reference books fail to explain the connection between the particular winged creatures and the gospels, but one expensive History of Christianity says:

> Matthew is represented by the winged man because he emphasized the incarnation of Jesus;
> Mark, by the lion, because he wrote of the royal lineage of Christ;
> Luke, by the ox, because he stressed the death and resurrection, and because the ox is the symbol of sacrifice;
> John, by the eagle, because of his great inspiration.

I find it hard myself to justify these explanations. Instead, we shall regard the symbols as traditional – a delightful tradition, however, in its outcome in art.

And now we shall hear three parables, each one special to its gospel. The first is from Mark, and here there is no choice, for there is only one parable peculiar to Mark; the second is from Luke and the third from Matthew and, in both cases, there is ample choice.

Reading

The first parable is told only by St Mark:

Jesus said, 'The kingdom of God is like this. A man scatters seed on the land; he goes to bed at night and gets up in the morning, and the seed sprouts and grows – how, he does not know. The ground produces a crop by itself, first the blade, then the ear, then full-grown corn in the ear; but as soon as the crop is ripe, he sets to work with the sickle, because harvest-time has come.'

Mark 4. 26–29 *NEB*

The second parable is told only by St Luke:

'Two men went up to the temple to pray, one a Pharisee and the other a tax-gatherer. The Pharisee stood up and prayed thus: "I thank thee, O God, that I am not like the rest of men, greedy, dishonest, adulterous; or, for that matter, like this tax-gatherer. I fast twice a week; I pay tithes on all that I get." But the other kept his distance and would not even raise his eyes to heaven, but beat upon his breast, saying, "O God, have mercy on me, sinner that I am." It was this man, I tell you, and not the other, who went home acquitted of his sins.'

Luke 18. 10–14a *NEB*

The third parable is told only by St Matthew:

'But what do you think about this? A man had two sons. He went to the first, and said, "My boy, go and work today in the vineyard." "I will, sir," the boy replied; but he never went. The father came to the second and said the same. "I will not," he replied, but afterwards he changed his mind and went. Which of these two did as his father wished?'

Matt. 21. 28–31a *NEB*

Let us pray

O God, we do not all believe, and those of us who do believe do not fully believe. Help us in our search for meaning. Help us to be true to what we already know.

And when we are perplexed and have no faith, give us grace to go on faithfully with our daily duties.

Teach us to love our neighbour as ourselves. Teach us to value service above self. Grant us sincerity of heart, that nothing in us may obscure the heavenly vision.

So may the seed sprout and grow though we know not how. And, when the harvest-time comes, may we be with the wheat that is gathered in, and not with the tares. Amen.

The Lord's Prayer

All   The grace of our Lord Jesus Christ,
    and the love of God,
    and the fellowship of the Holy Spirit,
be with us all evermore. Amen.

NOTES ON ASSEMBLIES 38-40

1. *Local investigations*

A group of students – perhaps the school's Local History Society, or the CEM group – should prepare for this series of assemblies by studying local churches and reading relevant literature. The references to Huddersfield churches in Assembly 39 indicate the kind of information which any locality can provide; references should obviously be local.

2. *Display material*

Art books open at plates showing the gospel symbols in ancient manuscripts should be on exhibition. It is possible that the Art Department could make replicas or copies of local instances of the four winged creatures. In Huddersfield, the window at St Paul's, Armitage Bridge, is suitable for copying, and use could be made of photography for this purpose.

3. *References*

Bible commentaries: Peake says, 'from the time of Irenaeus each of the creatures has been held to symbolize one of the four evangelists with very little point', and Gore speaks of 'their unfortunate identification with the four evangelists'. The words of Irenaeus quoted in Assembly 38 can be found in R. H. Bainton, *The History of Christianity* (Nelson, 1964), and this is the book referred to in Assembly 40. The exchange of symbols mentioned in Assembly 40 is explained under the heading 'Evangelist' in one of the volumes of *The Interpreter's Dictionary of the Bible* (Abingdon Press, Nashville).

4. XP

A fourth assembly, which could be added to these three, or could be separate, might be based on the chi-rho (XP). See *labarum* in any Encyclopedia.

5. *Art and Christianity*

A useful summary, *Symbols in Churches,* will be found at the end of the *AA* publication, *Treasures of Britain* (1968). Donald Whittle's *Christianity and the Arts* (Mowbray, 1966) is a useful first book on its theme for Sixth Formers.

FURTHER NOTES ON USING BIBLICAL MATERIAL

1. Notice should be taken of the Christian year; indeed this is implied in Assembly 29. The approach should not be 'devotional' so much as expositional. For instance, a December group of assemblies could be based on 'waiting for the consolation of Israel' (*Luke* 2. 25), introducing Old Testament ideas thematically.

2. When assemblies have the general character illustrated in this book, return to plain biblical narrative is enjoyed. I have used the following passages (with suitable introductions):

II *Sam.* 11. 1–9; 11. 14–12. 7; 12. 9–10, 13–24 (*RSV* or the *Jerusalem Bible*);
Jonah (the whole book in the *Knox* translation);
Judges 13. 2–5; 14; 15. 1–8 (*Knox*);
Judges 15. 8b–16. 30 (with Milton's *Samson Agonistes*, lines 81–109);
Job 1; 2; 3. 1–10 (*Knox*).

The style of the *Knox* translation sustains interest in longer-than-usual readings.

3. The great myths – of creation, and of the last judgment – and the problem of suffering, are at the centre of the biblical understanding of life, and should come into assemblies.

4. Psychological approaches (as instanced in Assemblies 9–12) can give immediate relevance to biblical incidents. In Acts, for instance, patterns of insincerity (Ananias, Simon, Sceva), and the links of the narrative with the epistles. Here, too, discussion of the various kinds of authority (*Mark* 1. 22), or the great words of religion

(see *A Theological Word Book of the Bible*, SCM Press, 1950), or the methods and kinds of prayer.

5. Another approach is through translations (from Tyndale onwards) and comments of translators (see the Introductions to E. V. Rieu's *The Four Gospels* and *The Acts of the Apostles* in the Penguin Classics, and J. B. Phillips, *Ring of Truth*, Hodder & Stoughton, 1967).

VI *Implications and Implementation*

There are several reasons for setting out fully the various acts of worship in this book. One is that a discussion of education through worship is impossible without illustrating what is meant. Such apparently small things as choice of words, methods of approach – hard to define without examples – make all the difference to mood and acceptability.

The fact is that many people make hasty judgments about school worship based on no better information than recollections of their own early experience. No one would judge current teaching of mathematics in this way, yet changes in method and outlook in religious education are as rapid as in mathematics, even though fewer people are fully equipped to effect them. Without a knowledge of what is happening now, whether in primary schools or in secondary schools, generalizations become out of date. This is the more serious, as we shall show, when so much that is important in education is at stake.

The reasons for giving special consideration to the Sixth Form are threefold. First, my own recent experience has been at this level – though equally in the Main School. However, it has been developments at the Sixth Form stage that have affected Main School worship, and not the reverse.

Secondly, I believe that if a corporate act of worship can be shown to be of value at the level of the Sixth Form – usually regarded as one of the most critical of audiences, as well as one of the most worthwhile – then it is likely that the problems of worship elsewhere in the school age-range will be soluble. I assume, here, that the Sixth Form can meet separately; problems are certainly greater when this is impossible. Indeed, one of the most difficult of 'congregations' is the one comprised of the full secondary-school range, from children of eleven to young men and women of nineteen, especially when this includes the full ability range too. In a church congregation of this sort there is at least a common religious interest and intent that can be taken for granted and which helps the presiding minister; this cannot be assumed in a school, though there should be a strong common community concern. Personally, I would advocate the breaking down of such a heterogeneous group into something more manageable so long as this is consistent with the social organization of the school. In any case, if the seniors are actively involved, if they find the act of worship educationally valuable, problems with their juniors will be eased.

But there is a third reason for the Sixth Form choice. The intellectual level is adult, and the content of greater intrinsic interest. In fact, the Sixth Form assembly can become a kind of forum – a whetstone on which the leader of assembly sharpens his own thinking. It provides a constant challenge to his powers of understanding, exposition, and empathy. And so, in this book, the worked-out acts of worship are more than illustrations; they are part of the developing argument. They become, with the accompanying notes, part of the text. Consequently, though any one group of these assemblies is typical of what goes on in a Sixth Form, taken consecutively they do not make a systematic course. Questions of balance and variety have to be considered and these matters have not been dealt with here (though they have in *Sixth Form Worship*).

What is the educational significance of school worship? Is the morning assembly no more than vestigial, a reminder, in a society becoming increasingly secular, that popular education was initially provided by the church? Or does it still serve the church, an out-post of her proselytizing mission though no longer manned by her personnel? Or does worship at the beginning of each day primarily serve the state by helping to maintain decent moral standards?

I think, in the first place, it is none of these things. The significance is an educational one, and this both by its *form* and by its *content*. There is, also, the professional's desire to do a good job in his profession. So long as a daily act of worship is required by law, many headmasters and their deputies, without further question, will do their best to make it worth while. But for some, what happens in assembly is of the essence of the educational process; this is the standpoint of this book.

First, as regards *form*: the bringing together each day of a school community which otherwise would not meet.

We have already referred to the cohesive effect of assembly, and to the importance of collective experience (p. 47). Both assume a measure of homogeneity – the feeling of a common purpose, or, the readiness to create such a feeling. Without this, assembling is no more than 'regimentation'. It is so regarded by senior pupils when its prime function appears to be to provide an occasion for school notices; modern techniques make possible much more efficient means of passing on information. And it is so regarded when the religious element is nominal and conventional and never quickens the spirit. But the content of the act of worship *can* minister to personal growth; it can be, in the fullest sense, educational. And then the assembly serves both the individual – in his own growth – and the group – making for social solidarity. This is why the full eleven to nineteen age range needs to be broken down, at any rate for some of the time, into communities of shared purpose and concern within the school.

A useful investigation (though this is not the place for it) would be to enquire into which attitudes and standards derive from and are fostered by membership of a self-educating community such as we have described, and which are individualistic. It may well prove that the atomization of society engendered by urbanization and industrialization needs to be countered in education by strengthening constructive group experience. Even the *form* of school worship can contribute here, the older fear of closed communities having long been exorcized. What is interesting to note is that, at a time of the 'eclipse of community' (the phrase is Bryan Wilson's), and of reluctance in the adult world to accept commitment, many educational developments are stressing individual response almost to the point of the parody, 'children must not be told anything, but must find out for themselves'. I am sure that these new approaches are necessary, but they do make the language of dissent easier to learn than the language of assent. Psychological well-being requires opportunity for team membership as well as for individual skills, humility before a body of knowledge as well as individual exploration.

But the daily assembly does more than provide occasion for one of the requirements of psychological growth – the feeling of belonging – it also helps create the community which makes belonging possible. Without this focus of collective pastoral concern, without this bringing together of the many sides of a school at the beginning of each day, social cohesion would break down. The school would tend to become an aggregate of departments, and pupils would arrive, as at a supermarket, to take from the counter what they thought useful to them, without any response of obligation to the whole. The corporateness of a good school is an essential part of its worth.

As regards *content*, the illustrative assemblies imply plenty of variety both of subject matter and of degree and kind of co-operation. But behind all this variety, behind the continuing concern with psychological growth and personal maturation, is a basic acceptance that life has *meaning* – a teleological element. Here is the essential content as was made explicit in Chapter III. We noted there the problems of the humanist in assembly and said he had a place alongside the Christian when both had in common 'a shared concern, commitment and intention' even though they articulated their awareness of the spiritual in different ways. Even so, the humanist has the more difficult problem of communication, both because he has no tradition in this respect, and because he approaches the task *de novo*.

The basic requirement is that *both* care about assembly and see its educational importance in the same way. The non-believer who does *not* attend assemblies does not so qualify. He would almost certainly assume a version of religion which the believer would not recognize, and would probably seek to undermine it.

The fact is, that in the school situation, participation arises not from any theoretical or explicitly expressed breadth of opinion, but from the nature of the job, from respect for people, and from recognition that each has something to offer to the maturing process. All this assumes acceptance of the educator's job as something that goes beyond instruction. And this is generally accepted if not always made explicit. Further, it is expected by the general public, as is shown by every outburst following youthful exuberance which takes anti-social forms!

But what kind of religion is this? It seems to be anchored neither in the churches nor in tradition, and agreed syllabuses do no more than recommend, they never define!

We have tried to lay bare the very minimum of 'belief'. Yet I think it *is* Christian, or, at any rate, pre-Christian rather than sub-Christian. It is not concerned to inculcate theological orthodoxy (though truth matters), nor to ensure institutional conformity (though membership of the school is valued), nor to recommend particular ritualistic practices (though attendance at worship is expected). It seeks to answer the spiritual needs of growing young people, and it is the product of caring.

Colin Alves, in *Religion and the Secondary School* (SCM Press, 1968), quotes Dr J. W. D. Smith:

Our 'image of God' may have to go but the religious dimension of life will always remain. The dawn of self-awareness confronts man with the mystery of his own nature and destiny. As boys and girls grow towards maturity they need to be helped to become aware of those depths in human existence and to make their own personal response to the reality which confronts them in that experience....

A secular society which refuses to acknowledge such problems is ignoring a vital educational task.

If 'school religion' develops an awareness of the religious dimension of life, then it provides a foundation on which churches can build if once they win the ear of young people. We shall say more later about the implications of this for churches. Sufficient, now, to say that, in assembly especially, a school seeks to meet religious needs because it recognizes religious needs, needs which cannot be ignored when helping young people to an adequate philosophy of life. Nevertheless, in a diversified society, a school cannot press particular answers; it can, however, hope to awaken a sympathy for and appreciation of the main Christian tradition. It is within this tradition that the school operates, for even the secularism of the Western world derives from Christianity and has Christian values embedded in it.

I remember an Indian friend describing himself as 'a Hindu in a Christian ethos'. And any description, even of unbelief, requires such a qualification. Perhaps that is why parents, and the public at large, continue to want to retain the religious element in maintained education. Despite the arguments of those humanists who see in 'compulsory religion' no more than improper indoctrination, and of those Christians who despair of school religion because so much of it is so poor, and because, in any case, it does not serve institutional religion – despite their arguments, the majority still want to retain religious 'instruction' and the daily act of worship. The demand does not arise from any love of the churches – most who make it are non-attenders and probably anti-clerical, nor from any affection for the particular form religious education has taken in the past. Nor is it only a desire for a moral prophylactic for the children, useful when they are young. I think there is a genuine feeling for something transcendental, some absolute in standards and values, some external yardstick, a law of God, which both justifies our intimations and hopes, and reproves our indifference. And even while remaining reproved, the feeling that it is not enough to educate 'clever devils'; that more is required than technological skills, and that, somehow, this 'more' lies within the province of religion, a religion divorced of accretions. We can neither afford to embrace it, nor to reject it; if we think about it at all the issues remain uneasily unresolved: let it have a place in education, perhaps the next generation will do better!

There is more in this than a nostalgia of lapsed Christians, more than a rueful acknowledgment by the spiritually inert. There is a sound intuition: life is not just 'a fortuitous concourse of atoms', there *is* 'a beyond in the midst'. When the educator includes religious education in the curriculum he is doing more than offering a sop to public demand, he is recognizing that when schools were released from a formal link with institutional religion they were not thereby released from concern with religious values. He is affirming that educational criteria go beyond knowledge and skills, beyond social and vocational requirements; they must include spiritual needs. He has, therefore, to give shape to this intuition and, in assembly, to be open-ended, 'if haply they might feel after him and find him, though he is not far from every one of us' (*Acts* 17. 27). This is what is at stake: whether the most typically human thing in life should be ignored, or whether room should be left open for its discovery.

So far we have assumed that there are two ways of looking at religion: in one, religion is of the individual, a light that lighteth every man, and here the psychology of growth can be illuminating; in the other, religion belongs to the institutional church with its traditions and bureaucratic apparatus, and here sociological considerations have value. But this description, which seems to oppose personal and institutional religion, is too simple. If it were insisted on, then we have also assumed that school religion is more concerned with the first than with the second, and so with the 'prophet' rather than with the 'priest', with the ministry of the Word rather than with the sacramental fellowship; and that there are historical and professional reasons for this. But the real situation is more complex, and not only because there is not 'the church', but only 'churches'. It calls for further analysis.

The fact is that education, like many of the social services, has its roots in the welfare work of the church, and conforms to the general pattern of development of most humanizing movements.

There is first the recognition of a social need and the response to it on a voluntary basis of both churchmen and other people of goodwill. Initially the response is one of personal service, regarded by church members as part of the outworking of their faith. The need, once it is recognized locally, may be seen to be widespread; but the response in action is often sporadic. Ultimately the matter may be taken up organizationally, as a special concern, by the whole church. The next stage begins when the state sees the value to the community of what is being done and supports it, usually by financial grants. These grants may be conditional on the maintenance of certain minimum standards of premises and equipment. In recent years the Youth Service in this country has gone through these two stages and passed on to the third, but personal counselling, as the trained but voluntary counsellors of the National Marriage Guidance Council understand it, has not yet got beyond Stage 2.

The third stage arrives when the state, realizing that it cannot depend on the accident of whether and where voluntary helpers are available, itself takes over responsibility to meet the need through its social services. At first, however, though making material provision, the state may be limited by its dependence on the philanthropic impulses of individuals for personnel, there being no other adequate motivation. A few paid workers may be placed discreetly to co-ordinate the voluntary activities of the public-spirited, though their emoluments may do little more than make it possible for their 'voluntary' service to be full-time. Nevertheless, this is the beginning of the professional in the service, and the developing of a corresponding expertise. Even when salaries become adequate, the service may not prove sufficiently attractive to ensure suitable recruitment except by appealing to a sense of vocation, perhaps because professional status has not yet been accorded.

The fourth stage sees the growth of a new profession, with entrance qualifications, training, and careers prospects. The amateur is now excluded. The word 'vocation' may remain for years, a reminder of how the service started, though there is no longer dependence on the church. It may, however, have to give way to 'profession', for the idea of 'vocation' may seem to put an improper obligation on people who do their job with professional pride and not as do-gooders. At the same time the 'need' ceases to be a need and becomes a right. 'Charity schools', and their equivalent in other spheres, disappear. In education, progress through the first three stages to the fourth can be seen accelerated in the one-time dependent territories as they achieve their own nationhood.

From the standpoint of religion this sketch can be viewed in various ways. It can be regarded as the story of the increasing secularization of all welfare work. True, it is the churches that were initially sensitive to human needs – but 'nothing fails like success'. The work is taken over by the state, layer after layer; it is beyond the churches' resources. The church becomes more and more irrelevant and retires into its own liturgical life. Contrariwise, religiously it may be regarded as a success story: The church is 'in the world' and the best Christian work of its members is in their daily work. The Christian cobbler serves his Lord by cobbling well. The distinction between 'secular' and 'sacred' breaks down. This is the leaven which leavens the lump.

There is more to say about it than this, but even this outline illuminates some of the difficulties of religious education in our schools. Further, it is from some such dichotomy in thinking that much of the uncertainty arises in churches about the meaning of 'mission'.

We shall consider how this analysis helps to explain current attitudes in education, and especially in religious education. Teaching in schools can never be completely 'secularized' if the religious needs of young people are to be met; certainly no other agency can cover these needs. Because this implies a pastoral side to the work of a teacher he can never be narrowly professional with a carefully delimited area of influence as could become the dead-end of Stage 4. In his specialism the schoolmaster is primarily a teacher, but in his pastoral role he is a person meeting the needs of persons in an environment whose sole purpose is their good. The headmaster's job is to hold a synoptic view of the whole educational process, and of all that influences his pupils, as it affects their growth; he cannot ignore the religious aspect. Open, he must be, in approach; uncertain, perhaps, he may be, of the insights he should mediate; but not indifferent to their fundamental importance.

The teacher's standard of excellence, however, even in religious education, lies *within* the area of his professional competence. It is seen in the enlargement of understanding in his pupils, not in their becoming affiliated with a local branch of the church. The lump is truly leavened when, by being true to itself, and not by deferring to some outside standard, even that of the church, it achieves its best work.

I have, myself, found that when educators meet in conference to discuss ends and means, and when their deliberations and group discussions are guided by Christians who, remaining professional, bring Christian insights to bear on their work, insights which prove to be no monopoly of the 'believer', then a kind of 'fellowship', unsought, can develop, which is truly religious, though the word 'religion' is not obtruded.

Nevertheless, there is often uncertainty of role as between the teaching profession and ministers of religion. To some extent this arises from lack of confidence on both sides – a lack of confidence because their distinct functions, methods, and aims have never been clearly defined. Too often, just because both use the word 'religious', their functions have been assumed to be identical, and they are not; or the teacher's role has been thought of as a watered down version of the minister's, and it is not. Only when these distinctions are clearly drawn and accepted will the way to equal co-operation be open; till then some mutual suspicion will be almost unavoidable. The proper word for the maintained school is not 'secularized', but something more like 'de-ecclesiasticized'!

Consider one aspect of the teacher's muddled disappointment. A church-going teacher is engaged in Religious Studies or in leading assembly, and he thinks of his work as important for the Kingdom of God, even though his aim is not to convert but rather to enlighten. His approach is quite different from that of the leader of a church group, and his purpose is different. Nevertheless, he thinks the church should be interested in his work, and he feels hurt that it is not. In all probability even the local Council of Churches will not be interested. Both organize their work without reference to the 'spadework' being done in the schools. But the same teacher might very well regard active expression of interest as intrusion. The visiting minister of religion is slightly suspect – he is taking advantage of a captive audience – he doesn't know the difference between preaching and teaching – he stands for a commitment which it would be wrong for a school to impose and, in any case, the regard afforded him comes from politeness, and not from an earned place in the school community. Alternatively, he may be so circumspect, so tentative, so unsure of himself in a teacher's world, that he is completely ineffective. Either way the confusion arises because roles are not clearly defined.

The established teacher may wryly observe that when a minister of religion comes into a school to do salaried part-time work as a member of the staff, it is better for him to teach a subject other than Religious Studies, at any rate until he becomes accepted by the Staff Room and by the boys. Only then will he be able to make his best contribution to Religious Studies. But this is only recognizing that ministerial training does not provide a teacher's expertise, and most ministers of religion would accept this. It is, however, an interesting fact that recent modifications in the course-content of university theological departments, and in A-level syllabuses, are in a direction which is likely to lead to better background knowledge for teaching Religious Studies.

It becomes clear that the teaching profession has to think with greater clarity about the place of Religious Studies and of worship in maintained schools set in a pluralist society, and about their function in this respect *vis-à-vis* organized religion. Those who oppose 'religion in schools' are often afraid of attitudes and assumptions which are now outdated and which no longer obtain, and which should have been left behind in education; they fail to see what is now at stake. At the same time many educators seek to incorporate Religious Studies into General Studies. It could then happen that the only specifically religious element would be the morning assembly.

In this chapter we have touched on many educational problems needing further investigation. We might sum up our comments by using Matthew Arnold's words about the Christian religion (recently quoted by Dr John A. T. Robinson): Men cannot do without it; they cannot do with it as it is. We have said that initiative must come from within the profession; it cannot come from elsewhere: Religious Studies teachers are not agents of institutional religion. We have implied that something like a Nuffield approach is required in school worship; the purpose is not to parade novelty, but to make basic things attractive. We have pointed to the need to define these basic things – the religious needs of growing children. We agree with the

Newsom Report comment (quoted also by Colin Alves in *Religion and the Secondary School*): 'The best schools give their pupils something... which they know they need when they receive it, though they had not realized the lack before.' Meanwhile the headmaster has to lead assembly tomorrow morning. He cannot wait for theoretical solutions; problems must be solved in action – tomorrow morning.

Appointments of headmasters are often made with scant regard for this most important aspect of their work. A concern for education implies interest in it, but not necessarily knowledge or experience. Where are these to come from? Or, if a headmaster delegates, how find a way of doing this without lessening his own status or stature in the school? Training for headmastering is becoming more common; it is important that alongside curricular and managerial aspects there should be due recognition of the function of a school which we have been discussing. Happy is the headmaster whose senior colleagues co-operate. So often heads of departments are reluctant to get away from the cosy known world of their specialism to this wider task. Perhaps they feel uneasily that they might compromise their own integrity; perhaps they do not want to commit themselves; perhaps they shrink from having to create an atmosphere of dignity; perhaps they are acutely aware of their lack of background knowledge. Or, maybe, it is just not their job. Yet we have shown how valuable participation is, both for the school, and for those involved.

Further, assembly makes other demands than those on the willingness and time of teachers. In a Sixth Form of 250 boys, assembly for ten minutes per day involves as many boy-hours as does six periods per week for sets of twenty boys doing Physics in the two years. Few schools will spend as much of their resources of time and money on preparation for each. But school worship should not be starved of reference books, music, equipment, and the various tools of the job.

This book is an argument for school worship – not a disputation but, at a particular level, a demonstration. It shows what would be lost if school worship were to disappear – all that the assemblies set out in this book seek to do. I hope, too, that it clarifies issues, for it presents the 'religious' part of the teacher's task as essentially educational, meeting the needs of children, and not as an ancillary of organized religion.

Almighty God, Father of all men, who hast given us by thy Son the good news of thy kingdom, grant that we may day by day have a fuller understanding of all that it means, and of the work we must do in it, that we may feel ourselves filled with a common purpose as fellow-workers with thee and each other, for the extension of that same kingdom, through Jesus Christ our Lord.

Source not known

Our Father, which art in heaven, hallowed be thy name. Thy kingdom come. Thy will be done in earth as it is in heaven. Give us this day our daily bread. And forgive us our trespasses, as we forgive them that trespass against us. And lead us not into temptation, but deliver us from evil. For thine is the kingdom, the power, and the glory, for ever and ever.   Amen.

> The grace of our Lord Jesus Christ,
>   and the love of God,
>   and the fellowship of the Holy Spirit,
> be with us all evermore.   Amen.

ACKNOWLEDGMENTS

I am grateful to the following for their kind permission to quote extracts from the works named:

The Delegates of the OUP and the Syndics of the CUP for the passages from the *New English Bible*.

The Division of Christian Education of the National Council of the Churches of Christ in the USA for the passages from the *Revised Standard Version*.

The Cardinal Archbishop of Westminster for the passages from the Ronald Knox translation of the Bible.

Hodder & Stoughton Ltd for the passages from *The New Translation of the Bible* by John Moffatt.

George Allen & Unwin Ltd for the passage from *The Conquest of Happiness* by Bertrand Russell.

The BBC for the prayers from *New Every Morning*.

Blackie and Son Ltd for poems from *The Keen Edge* by Jack Beckett.

The Cambridge University Press for the passages from *The Nature of the Physical World* by A. S. Eddington.

Jonathan Cape and the Executors of the author for passages from *The Book of Beasts* by T. H. White.

Collins Publishers for a passage from *The Historical Jesus* by Heinz Zahrnt.

Faber & Faber Ltd for a passage from *Murder in the Cathedral* by T. S. Eliot.

Mr Michael Flanders for permission to quote words from *A Song of Patriotic Prejudice* as sung in *At the Drop of Another Hat* by him and Donald Swann who composed the music (Parlophone PCS 3052).

The executors of the James Joyce Estate for a passage from *A Portrait of the Artist as a Young Man* by James Joyce published by Jonathan Cape.

Methuen & Co. Ltd for a passage from *The Making of Victorian England* by G. Kitson Clark.

Oxford University Press for the prayers from *Daily Prayer* compiled by Eric Milner-White and G. W. Briggs; and for the passage from the preface to *The Christian Teaching* in Vol. 12 of the Centenary Edition of *The Works of Leo Tolstoy* from the Maude translations of Tolstoy.

SCM Press Ltd for prayers from *A Book of Prayers for Schools*; and for the passages from *Honest to God* by J. A. T. Robinson and *Two Refugees* by D. S. Russell & M. R. Bielby.

SPCK for a prayer from *A Book of Prayers for Everyman*.

I have tried to trace prayers, etc., to their original sources, but if any copyright has been infringed unknowingly, I beg the owner's pardon.